ONE NATION UNDER GOD

ONE NATION UNDER GOD

Ten Things Every Christian Should Know
About the Founding of America

Dr. David C. Gibbs, Jr.
with
Jerry Newcombe

Christian Law Association
PO Box 4010
Seminole, FL 33775-4010
www.christianlaw.org

The Work and Ministry of

The Christian Law Association

The Christian Law Association is a "ministry of legal helps." Its purpose is to provide legal assistance to Bible-believing churches and Christians who are experiencing legal difficulty in practicing their religious faith. CLA represents churches, schools, individuals and a wide variety of ministries.

CLA is funded wholly by concerned Christians and churches who wish to support the fight for religious liberty in the United States, and who also have a desire to make it possible for CLA to provide cost-free legal assistance to Bible-believing churches and Christians who are being sued, or threatened with suit, for the Biblical faith.

Since 1969, when CLA began, the demand for assistance has exploded. CLA received in excess of 100,000 requests for assistance in this past year.

CLA serves through the following ways:

- Free legal defense of those facing difficulties for the Biblical faith
- Free legal counsel to churches and Christians for their ministries
- Legal seminars for ministries to help prevent lawsuits
- The *Legal Alert* radio program broadcast on over one thousand stations around the world
- Legal books and other resources to inform Christians of their rights
- Preaching in churches across the country
- Publication of a monthly newsletter, *The Legal Alert*
- Free legal consulting to local, state, and federal officials and legislators to provide maximum religious liberty
- Intercessory prayer ministry for requests sent to the ministry offices

As a faith-based ministry, CLA appreciates the prayers and financial support of our friends and the opportunity to serve wherever needed.

If the ministry of the Christian Law Association can legally serve you in any way, it would certainly be our honor and delight to do so. We can be contacted at the address on the opposite page.

All Scripture quotations are from the *Holy Bible, King James Version.*

Published by the Christian Law Association, P.O. Box 4010, Seminole, Florida 33775-4010 www.christianlaw.org

First Edition 2003

Second Edition 2005

Front cover image:
Declaration of Independence, by John Trumbull,
courtesy of the Architect of the Capitol.
Back cover image:
American flag with 13 stars,
courtesy of the Daughters of the American Revolution Museum.

Design and Production: Design4 Marketing Communication, Inc.

Printed in the United States of America

This book is dedicated

to the outstanding men and women who make up the

legal missionary team at the Christian Law Association.

Faithfully, they work to defend the freedoms

of churches and Christians across our nation.

*"Blessed is the nation whose God is the LORD; and the
people whom he hath chosen for his own inheritance."*
~ Psalm 33:12

CONTENTS

Foreword by D. James Kennedy, Ph.D.

Introduction: Two Competing Truths

ONE NATION
UNDER GOD

Foreword

The Scripture says, "Blessed is the nation whose God is the Lord." The Bible asks, "if the foundations be destroyed, what shall the righteous do?" Anyone who looks at the facts about America will see that this was founded as a Christian nation.

There is no doubt that this is a nation which was built upon the Christian faith – that the Lord, indeed, was the God of this nation, that it was founded upon the principles of God's Word, upon the teachings of Christianity, and for the advancement of the Kingdom of Christ. All of these things are well-documented, in the charters of the original colonies, in the original compacts (like the famous Mayflower Compact), covenants, and constitutions. When the Supreme Court looked into the matter in 1892, poring over all the original documents, they concluded with one unanimous, unambiguous voice: "this is a Christian nation."

All nations that have ever existed have been founded upon some theistic principle – either some theistic or anti-theistic principle – whether we think of the Hinduism of India, the Confucianism of China, the Mohammedanism of Saudi Arabia, or the atheism of the former Soviet Union. When we think of America, if we know our history, we know that this was a nation founded upon Christ and His Word. Those foundations, indeed, are crumbling in our time.

All of this is under enormous attack and has been for the last few decades. In fact, so effective has been the attack that the historical revisionists have all but removed every vestige of our Christian heritage from the textbooks in our schools. There are those in our country today who are busily tearing apart that foundation who would gnash their teeth at the idea that this is a Christian nation, and will not be satisfied until they have removed every vestige of our Christian heritage from not only the minds, but also the monuments of this country.

These outspoken secularists have tried to rob us of our rich Christian heritage. The history books have been rewritten, and God has been erased.

Yet it is impossible to tell America's true history if you erase the Christian heritage. This nation was founded by Christians largely for Christian purposes. The facts of history cannot be so easily erased.

The facts of history are what this new book is all about. In page after page, it is very clear that we began as a Christian nation, and that here lies the key to our national greatness. Since the beginning of the 1970s, Attorney David Gibbs, Jr. has been fighting for religious liberty as an attorney – as a legal missionary. For this book, he has teamed up with Jerry Newcombe, who has co-authored some books with me, including the bestseller, *What If Jesus Had Never Been Born?* Together, they have culled the facts of history and have assembled ten indisputable facts that every Christian should know about the founding of this great land. I recommend it highly.

It's high time we reclaim our Christian heritage before it's too late. May God use this book to help in that worthy goal.

~ D. James Kennedy, Ph.D.

Introduction
Two Competing Truths

"... where the Spirit of the Lord is, there is liberty."
~ 2 Corinthians 3:17

America was founded as one nation under God, but in our modern day, many of these remembrances are disappearing rapidly as a new spirit of secularism continues to sweep across our land. Daily, I watch assaults on our religious liberty from various sectors and on various fronts. Some secular groups are doing everything possible to remove any vestige of Christianity from our nation's culture. These people are dedicated to extracting any reference to God, the Bible, or Jesus Christ from our history and from American public life. Unfortunately, in many cases, their efforts toward this end have been very effective.

More than thirty years ago, there was a growing hostility against Christianity and religious liberty brewing in the land that I never anticipated. I never believed that in America a Christian could be sued or threatened with a lawsuit for doing what was Biblically right. As I grew up, these types of problems were unimaginable, but as a Christian adult, trained to be an attorney, I could not ignore calls for help from pastors and churches. So, while practicing law for a living, I began to defend Christians who were experiencing legal difficulties because of their Biblical faith.

My firm and I as "legal missionaries" were beginning to defend pastors, churches, and individual Christians who were being hauled before the courts of America for practicing their Biblical faith. This discrimination was happening at an unbelievable pace.

We had no money. My car had 146,000 miles on the odometer and no gas in the fuel tank. Our law firm had spent every dime it had to help churches and Christians free of charge. It was becoming apparent that the battle against Christians in America was larger than anyone had initially anticipated.

The Christian Law Association, CLA, was born in those days to raise support for our legal ministry of helps to Bible-believing churches. CLA was premised on the idea that for American Christians to remain free to practice their faith, believers nationwide had to band together and help. God's people have been faithful through the years to do their part to make sure the flame of American liberty would not be quenched.

Today the Christian Law Association receives more than 65,000 phone calls annually from Christians requesting legal help to practice their faith. The cases are shocking:

> *"There is an all-out assault now on the Christian community in this country."*
>
> Rush Limbaugh,
> Radio Talk Show Host

• A pastor sued for what he preached.

• A church sued for trying to build on its own property.

• A Christian in the workplace told that he cannot mention Jesus Christ or display anything in his private work area that would denote faith in Him.

• A wayward teenager using the force of government to break the spiritual values being taught in the home.

As legal missionaries, we are obligated to help these people. And by the grace of God, we are able to do that. Yet, since our nation began with such a uniquely Christian heritage, I am amazed that America has fallen to such a state.

The forces of secularism are hard at work in an attempt to strip from our culture every last vestige of America's Christian heritage. Even worse, they are threatening our religious freedom – the very reason so many religious dissidents originally came to these shores. Our forefathers created out of this new land a haven for religious freedom and freedom of conscience. But today, these precious freedoms are in jeopardy. For example, consider some of the following calls our office at the Christian Law Association has responded to by providing legal assistance.

Discrimination in Education
Education is one of the largest battlefields for religious liberty today.

Attorneys for CLA are called upon to intervene in situations where Christians are discriminated against every day of the week. Our cases involve defense of Christian schools, as well as defense of Christian children in public schools. Some examples:

• Two homosexuals filed an employment discrimination complaint against a church preschool program after they were dismissed when they revealed their sexual orientation.

• Public school students were told they would be expelled if they talked about Jesus in school.

• A world culture teacher brought in an outside speaker to present the Muslim faith to students, but refused to provide the same access for a Christian speaker.

• A public high school student failed a test because he refused to answer a question asking students to prove the scientific falsity of the Biblical claim that Moses parted the Red Sea.

• School officials planned to place a public school student in detention because she brought her Bible to school.

• A student was told she could not place a Ten Commandments poster on her public school locker even when other children were permitted to post secular posters of their choice on their lockers.

• A Christian student was told he could not read his Bible during independent reading time in public school. He was also told he could not read a Christian magazine or even a book about the Constitution and Christian values.

> *"We may fail to teach our students the rudiments of literature, science, and history. Twenty percent of high-school graduates may be functional illiterates, or semi-literate. We may be unable to maintain even a semblance of order in our urban schools, which increasingly resemble happy hour in Beirut. But, hallelujah, we sure know how to protect kids from God."*
>
> Syndicated columnist
> Don Feder

• University students were prohibited from mentioning Jesus by name in an advertisement for their Christian group, while school authorities did not censor the ads of secular groups.

• Members of a Christian club were told their group could not meet unless they agreed to permit non-Christians to be elected to the club leadership. Other clubs were permitted to limit membership (and leadership) to students who shared their objectives.

• A state education department attempted to ban a Christian science curriculum because it taught creation as well as evolution.

Discrimination in the Workplace

Another area where many conflicts occur over religion is in the workplace. CLA receives an ever-increasing number of calls each week from employees who have been discriminated against by their employers because of their Biblical faith. The following is a sampling of some of the workplace calls we have received:

• A government employee was reprimanded for decorating her office door with religious symbols during an Easter door-decorating contest.

• A federal employee was not allowed to place religious material on a book rack specifically reserved for employees to share reading material during breaks.

• A worker was reprimanded for reading his Bible when work stopped during a tornado warning, even though other employees were allowed to read newspapers and secular books.

• An employee at a large bottling company was told he could no longer bring his Bible into the plant to read quietly to himself on his lunch break because other employees were offended by seeing it. This employee was also told to stop bringing a copy of a daily devotional booklet to share with a co-worker, despite the fact that these two workers had regularly shared such material for over a year.

Discrimination in the Public Square

The workplace and the field of education are not the only public arenas in which Christian speech and values are being challenged. The Christian message is becoming increasingly unwelcome, even in traditional public forum areas where speech, including religious speech, has previously been constitutionally protected. Regulations increasingly attempt to prohibit Christians from presenting their message on public street corners and in the public parks of America. For instance:

• One state supreme court upheld a local regulation permitting businesses to have street preachers arrested if their message was loud enough to be heard inside the buildings.

• A local government attempted to outlaw religious displays in some public parks.

• Libraries and public schools, as well as community centers all across the nation, are becoming less inclined to make their facilities available to Christians on the same basis as they do for secular community groups.

Discrimination in Zoning

Zoning regulations have become a growing concern for ministry leaders who contact the Christian Law Association. When zoning first became popular in America in the early 20th century, churches were rarely adversely affected by local zoning codes.

Traditionally, churches were located in residential communities. They were seldom zoned out of any area because society presumed that churches were good for the community. Even nonreligious citizens, until just a few decades ago, generally

> *"The perception now is that the Constitution requires that we purge all religion from the public square."*
>
> Nathan A. Forrester,
> The Beckett Fund for
> Religious Liberty

believed religion was a good thing for society. Today, zoning codes have become problems for churches because this earlier American respect for religion is disappearing.

Local government officials now more often look upon churches with suspicion. Today, the deference local communities once extended to churches is no longer automatic. Here are some of the problems CLA callers describe with respect to how zoning laws affect their churches and schools:

• Churches are excluded from commercial districts. This is often because local communities are reluctant to permit tax-exempt entities to "take away" commercial real estate that could remain on the tax rolls.

• Churches are excluded from various zoning districts even when other nonreligious assembly uses are permitted.

• Churches are unreasonably limited in how they may use the property and facilities they own.

• Home Bible studies are being limited and, in some cases, even declared illegal and shut down.

• One city barred a couple from holding more than one prayer meeting in their home each month.

• Local administrative officials proposed limiting the operational hours of some churches.

These situations would have been unthinkable a generation ago, but the modern forces of secularism in America are increasingly focused on omitting any vestige of religion from the public square. It is obvious, however, that some of these examples go beyond the public square and right into our private homes.

> "Christian bashing is a popular indoor sport."
>
> Pat Buchanan,
> Syndicated Columnist

Discrimination in Other Arenas

Complaints have been made against Christian expression in many areas:

• One Christian was told he could not display the Ten Commandments in front of his trailer in a mobile home park because the display would offend atheist residents.

• A woman was told by her homeowners' association board that her Christian Bible study group could not meet in the community meeting room even though other social groups regularly met there.

• Senior citizens were told they could not say grace before eating a common meal in a state-run senior center.

• A hostess at a theme park was told it was against federal law to mention the name of Jesus in the park. She was told she would be terminated immediately if she mentioned that name again in the park, despite all those who routinely took Jesus Christ's name in vain and were not threatened with termination.

Censorship of the Christian message in history books and in the public square is ominous. America's founders were adamant in their views that only a religious people could maintain the liberty given to them by God and enshrined by them in the Declaration of Independence.

The Reason for This Book

There are two competing philosophies or worldviews in modern America. On the one hand, America retains the rich Godly heritage that originally made her great. On the other hand, secularists are increasingly putting at risk both our heritage and the religious liberties of all Americans.

Although traders, explorers and businessmen also had a hand in the founding of America, historical revisionists cannot erase the fact that the first people who founded colonies in this land were primarily religious nonconformists. The reason for this book is to educate and inform the Christian public about ten important things every Christian ought to know about the founding of America.

1) Christopher Columbus, who opened up the New World to the Old, was motivated by his Christian faith to make his difficult voyage.

2) In 1620, the Pilgrims drafted our nation's first self-governing document, the Mayflower Compact. In that document, the Pilgrims clearly stated that they came to the New World to glorify God and to advance the Christian faith.

> *"... those nations only are blessed whose God is the Lord."*
>
> Abraham Lincoln,
> 16th President

3) The Puritans, who followed the Pilgrims to New England, created Bible-based commonwealths in order to practice a representative government that was modeled on their church covenants. Their more than one hundred governmental covenants and compacts essentially laid the foundation for America's Constitution, which was drafted in 1787 and ratified in 1789.

4) Various settlements throughout the early colonies provided refuge for religious dissidents of all types, the most famous being those founded by Roger Williams in Rhode Island and William Penn in Pennsylvania.

5) The education of the settlers and founders of America was uniquely Christian and Bible-based. Our Founding Fathers all received a thoroughly Christian education at all levels. All America's early universities – including Harvard, William and Mary, Yale, and Princeton – were Biblically Christian in their origins. Rare was the American of 1776 who did not know the Scriptures.

6) The Great Awakening was a key factor in uniting the separate

pre-Revolutionary War colonies and in increasing communication among them. As evangelists like George Whitefield roamed up and down the eastern seaboard preaching the Gospel, a religious revival occurred that drew the thirteen colonies together spiritually. As clashes between Great Britain and America increased, these colonists sought peace with Mother England, but not at the price of compromising their convictions.

7) The colonial pulpits, especially in New England, played a pivotal role in encouraging independence from Britain. The Minutemen were generally members of local churches, organized by their pastor or head deacon. The pastors' sermons, especially just before election day, informed the people about what was happening politically and what they, as faithful Christians, should do about it.

8) Christianity played a very important role in bringing about American Independence, including shaping the thinking of President George Washington and other early American heroes such as Samuel Adams, sometimes called the lightning rod of the American Revolution, and Patrick Henry, its great orator.

9) The Declaration of Independence was based on Christian ideas and viewpoints. The liberties it granted to citizens were understood to come directly from the God of the Bible.

10) The Biblical understanding of the sinfulness of man was the guiding principle behind the United States Constitution. The Bible was quoted more than any other source in the political writings of America's founding era. In the First Amendment, the founders presented America with a framework for religious liberty, not a weapon to be used by secularists against any public expression of Christianity.

Let us explore the true history of this great and unique nation.

America the Beautiful

Survey the history of the world, and you will never find another nation like the United States of America. America has become the world's lone super-power, the model nation that many try to emulate. More constitutions are based on ours than on any other. We are the envy of the world. Many hopeful immigrants risk their lives to come to these shores.

What is the source of America's greatness? We are great because of our rich Christian heritage. In a very real way, North America began in 1620 "in the name of God," as the Mayflower Compact, our very first self-governing document, clearly proclaims.

In the early 1830's, a Frenchman came to America to investigate how our nation dealt with prisoners. Instead, he expanded his study and wrote a two-part book about his general observations entitled *Democracy in America*. Amazingly, after some 170 years, Alexis de Tocqueville's book is still in print. In the opening of his second volume, de Tocqueville reminds us: "It must never be forgotten that religion gave birth to Anglo-American society." [1]

G.K. Chesterton was a popular writer who lived in the early part of the 20th century in England. In an essay entitled, "What I Saw in America," he made this observation: "America is the only nation in the world that is founded on a creed. That creed is set forth with dogmatic and even theological lucidity in the Declaration of Independence." [2]

> *The Bible "is the rock on which our Republic rests."*
>
> Andrew Jackson,
> 7th President

The eminent British historian, Paul Johnson, author of *Modern Times*, had this to say about our country in his excellent book, *A History of the American People*:

> The creation of the United States of America is the greatest of all human adventures. . . . [T]he Americans originally aimed to build an other-worldly "City on a Hill," but found themselves designing a republic of the people, to be a model for the entire planet. [3]

In short, ours is a peculiar country with a unique history. What is best in America can be traced back to our Judeo-Christian heritage. What is problematic in our nation is our departure from that heritage.

A Quick Survey

The Jamestown adventurers arrived in Virginia in 1607; and, although their colony was initially fraught with difficulties, one of their purposes had been to bring the Gospel to the New World. When the Pilgrims set sail for Virginia in 1620, they were blown off course and established Plymouth, Massachusetts, as the first Christian colony in America. Forty-one Pilgrims signed the Mayflower Compact on November 11, 1620, and declared their intention to establish this colony in God's name and for His glory, and to advance the Christian faith.

Beginning in 1630, thousands of Puritans under the leadership of John Winthrop followed the Pilgrims to the New World. It was their desire to achieve these objectives:

• Carry the Gospel and bring the fullness of the Gentiles into the Kingdom of God.

• Enjoy the liberties of the Gospel in purity with peace.

• Obey the Great Commission of Matthew 28:19, 20 to share the Gospel with the American Indians and with thousands of souls in transit across the ocean who needed to hear about Jesus.

• Help establish and support an infant church.

• Be a city on a hill, a city of God, a holy city in America.

> *"Finally, let us not forget the religious character of our origin. Our fathers were brought hither by their high veneration for the Christian religion. They journeyed by its light, and labored in its hope. They sought to incorporate its principles with the elements of their society, and to diffuse its influence through all their institutions, civil, political, or literary."*
>
> Daniel Webster,
> 19th Century
> American political leader

In 1636, Roger Williams left the Massachusetts Bay colony and dedicated Providence, Rhode Island, as a shelter for religious nonconformists. The Rhode Island Charter of 1663 later expressed in writing his evangelistic spirit toward Native Americans, an attitude he shared with the Pilgrims:

[W]hereby our said people and inhabitants, in the said Plantations, may be so religiously, peaceably and civilly governed, as that, by their good life and orderly conversations, they may win and invite the native Indians of the country to the knowledge and obedience of the only true God, and Savior of mankind. [4]

In 1637, Queen Christina of Sweden granted a colonial charter to encourage trade, settlement and the spreading of the Gospel in Delaware. Later, in 1642, she gave instructions regarding Christian living for the colony:

Above all things, shall the Governor consider and see to it that a true and due worship, becoming honor, laud, and praise be paid to the Most High God in all things, and to that end all proper care shall be taken that divine service be zealously performed . . . and all persons, but especially the young, shall be duly instructed in the articles of their Christian faith; and all good church discipline shall in like manner be duly exercised and received.

The wild nations, bordering upon all other sides, the Governor shall . . . at every opportunity, exert himself, that the same wild people may gradually be instructed in the truths and worship of the Christian religion.[5]

In 1639, the Colony of Connecticut adopted a set of Fundamental Orders in which the inhabitants agreed to govern themselves according to the laws of God in order to maintain and preserve the liberty and purity of the Gospel of the Lord Jesus Christ that they professed.

In 1677, the Quaker Trustees of West Jersey (later called Pennsylvania) established a government whose framework made provision for the people's liberty as Christians of all sects. The Charter provided for complete freedom of worship.

In 1681, William Penn provided a haven in Pennsylvania for Quakers and for all those professing Jesus as the Christ and Savior. He established a community based on both political and religious freedom that would be an example to the nations. Viewing his colony as a "Holy Experiment," Penn wanted to establish a society that was both Godly and virtuous and to bring "the savage natives by gentle and just manners to the Love of Civil Societ[y] and Christian religion."[6]

One of the goals of the Georgia Trustees under James Oglethorpe in 1733 was to provide for the conversion of the Indians through the colony's good discipline and example of just, moral, and religious behavior. Oglethorpe's first official act as a Trustee in Savannah was to kneel with his company to offer thanksgiving and prayer to God.

Conclusion

It is clear when we review our nation's history that it began as a nation under God. It is important for Christians to remember that fact if we are to continue to preserve our faith and our liberties.

Chapter 1

Christopher – *the "Christ-Bearer"* – Columbus

"And this gospel of the kingdom shall be preached in all the world for a witness unto all nations; and then shall the end come."
~ Matthew 24:14

Christopher Columbus was motivated by his Christian faith to sail to the New World.

I n 1492, Christopher Columbus set sail westward from Spain and forever changed the course of world history. But the modern world appears to have forgotten the true motivation for this historic voyage. The first thing every Christian should know about the founding of America is that Christopher Columbus, who opened up the New World to the Old, was motivated by his Christian faith to make his difficult voyage.

Today Christopher Columbus (1451-1506) is a man both praised and vilified, honored and ridiculed. Was he a visionary explorer or just an opportunistic exploiter? We must be careful to avoid both extremes in our assessment. Some today completely denigrate Columbus for all the shameful deeds of those who followed him. Others exalt him as if he were a totally noble character. In reality, Columbus was a flawed man, but he was also a visionary. Most importantly, he had a very strong commitment to the Christian faith.

Columbus' voyage was certainly "the most memorable maritime enterprise in the history of the world."[1] That is the assessment of George Bancroft (1800-1891), the first great American historian, who wrote a multi-volume history of our country that stood as the standard for at least half a century. Bancroft is not as widely read today, possibly in part because he did not censor out the Christian roots of our nation. We will be referencing Bancroft often in this book, however, because he was much closer to the original documents and sources than are modern historians.

God used Columbus, the Genoan sailor, to boldly venture into unknown territory. Any reasonable study of his life shows that Christopher Columbus was a man who loved the Scriptures and found his motivation in them. The verse quoted at the opening of this chapter ("And this gospel of the kingdom shall be preached in all the world for a witness unto all nations; and then shall the end come," Matthew 24:14) was very important to him. Columbus hoped his historic voyage would help bring about the return of Christ to the world.

> *"My hope in the One who created us all sustains me: He is an ever present help in trouble . . . "*
>
> Christopher Columbus,
> *Book of Prophecies*

Hero to Villain

Columbus was previously considered to be one of the greatest heroes in American history. More cities, streets, and towns are named for him than almost any historical figure other than Washington and Lincoln. He has been depicted in stone all across this land. Even the Pledge of Allegiance was created to honor the 400th anniversary of Christopher Columbus' discovery of America. The Pledge was written by a Baptist minister, Francis Bellamy (1856-1931) of Boston.[2] Rev. Bellamy wrote the Pledge in 1892 for school children across the nation to recite as the American flag was raised during the 400th anniversary celebrations.

Now that the 500th anniversary of Columbus' discovery of America has come and gone, some Americans condemn both the man and the holiday. They seek to depict Columbus as a murderous pirate who brought death and slavery to the New World, killing Native Americans by ill treatment and disease.

Consider some of the feelings Columbus now evokes:

> • The Mayor of Berkeley, California, announced on the eve of the 500th anniversary of Columbus Day that the city would no longer celebrate it. Instead, October 12 was proclaimed to be "Indigenous Peoples Day."[3] However, since one can never be politically correct enough, the mayor had to quickly add: "[T]his is in no way a slap at Italians."[4]

• The National Council of Churches has decried "the genocide, slavery, ecocide, and exploitation that followed in Columbus' wake."[5]

• Russell Means, a Native American activist, had extremely harsh words for the Italian explorer: "Columbus makes Hitler look like a juvenile delinquent. He was a racist, a mass murderer, a slave trader, a rapist, and a plunderer."[6] But modern revisionists notwithstanding, Christopher Columbus depicted himself as a servant of God.

The Pledge Also Under Attack

The Pledge of Allegiance, written to commemorate the 400th anniversary of Columbus' voyage, has come under attack today by some of the very same groups that have vilified Christopher Columbus. Some people now find the Pledge offensive, particularly because of the phrase "under God," which was added by Congress in 1954. President Dwight D. Eisenhower said at the time he signed that law:

> *"A funny thing happened on the way to the quincentennial observation of America's discovery: Columbus got mugged."*
>
> Columnist Gary Wills

FROM THIS DAY FORWARD, the millions of our school children will daily proclaim in every city and town, every village and rural school house, the dedication of our nation and our people to the Almighty. To anyone who truly loves America, nothing could be more inspiring than to contemplate this rededication of our youth, on each school morning, to our country's true meaning.[7]

A year later, in 1955, President Eisenhower said again:

Without God, there could be no American form of Government, nor an American way of life. Recognition of the Supreme Being is the first – the most basic – expression of Americanism. Thus the founding fathers of America saw it, and thus with God's help, it will continue to be.[8]

In the summer of 2002, many Americans were shocked when a federal appellate court declared that it was unconstitutional to recite the Pledge of Allegiance in public schools because of the phrase, "under God." That decision, although still under review, should serve as a wake-up call for all Americans, signaling what the federal judiciary has been doing little by little over the last fifty years in its reinterpretation of the Establishment Clause of the First Amendment.

Interestingly, the whole federal Pledge case that this plaintiff used in an attempt to strip away America's Judeo-Christian heritage was based on a false factual premise. Michael Newdow, the atheist who filed the lawsuit, claimed that his second-grade daughter was offended just by hearing the words "under God" spoken in her classroom (children may not be required to recite the Pledge in violation of their religious beliefs). This experience, he claimed, was causing his daughter psychological damage. The reality was that Mr. Newdow was estranged from his daughter's mother (they had never married), and both the daughter and mother attended church. In reality, the little girl liked to say the Pledge of Allegiance and wanted to continue to honor God.

> *"Ridiculous . . . out of step with the history and traditions of America . . ."*
>
> President George W. Bush's reaction to the June 2002 court decision, declaring the Pledge of Allegiance unconstitutional

Apart from the dubious facts of this case, the legitimacy of the decision is also dubious. The real irony of the California Pledge case is that Mr. Newdow, the plaintiff, does not seem to realize that the only reason he is permitted to be an atheist without penalty in the United States is because the right to believe or not to believe was granted to him in America under the authority of the very God he is seeking to censor.

The decision to ban the Pledge of Allegiance as unconstitutional, however, was a natural outgrowth of other modern cases based on the Establishment Clause. Judges today have misunderstood and misapplied the phrase "separation of church and state" to the Establishment Clause in a misguided attempt to legally ban any reference to God in the public arena, an action our Founding Fathers would not have understood or approved. Unfortunately, this Pledge decision was the erroneous but logical legal outcome of the last fifty years of Establishment Clause jurisprudence.

Columbus Day

We need to take a moment and look at the bigger picture. It becomes clear as we witness attacks on both Christopher Columbus and the Pledge of Allegiance that the real target is Western Civilization and, in some cases, Christianity itself. Until very recently, honoring Columbus and reciting the Pledge of Allegiance with hand over heart were both associated with patriotism and love of God and country.

Columbus Day was established to honor Christopher Columbus for his discovery of America on October 12, 1492. In describing this discovery to King Ferdinand of Spain, Columbus portrayed himself as a devout and sincere Christian who rejoiced in the souls that would be saved in this new land. He wrote:

> Therefore let the king and queen, the princes and their most fortunate kingdoms, and all other countries of Christendom give thanks to our Lord and Saviour Jesus Christ, who has bestowed upon us so great a victory and gift. Let religious processions be solemnized; let sacred festivals be given; let the churches be covered with festive garlands. Let Christ rejoice on earth, as he rejoices in heaven, when he foresees coming to salvation so many souls of people hitherto lost.[9]

We do not know how Columbus' news was actually celebrated in the 15th Century, but we do know that thousands of European Christians followed Columbus to America to plant colonies and lead souls to Christ.

> *"Obviously, the liberal court in San Francisco has gotten this one wrong."*
>
> The Honorable Dennis Hastert, Speaker of the House on the 2002 Pledge decision

Guilt by Association

It is certainly true that some Europeans who followed Columbus to the New World mistreated the Native American populations. In fact, the Catholic priest, Bartholomew de Las Casas, was vehement in rebuking the conquistadors for their unchristian behavior.[10] Relationships between the Indians and the settlers were complicated; however, we must remember, that those religious dissidents who sought to Christianize the Indians generally treated them far more humanely than did the conquistadors.

While we clearly cannot condone the barbarism and exploitation of early European explorers, we must also realize that it was other Europeans who introduced Christianity to the New World and thus sowed the seeds for positive change and deliverance in many of the Indian populations. It is a common mistake to blame Columbus for all the sins – perceived and real – committed by all Europeans following his voyage.

Dr. John Eidsmoe in his book, *Columbus and Cortez*, gives us one explanation for the recent revisionist political movement that is attempting to defame this great seafaring visionary. He says: "[S]ome are determined to remake America into a secular or pagan society. To do so, they must move this nation away from its Christian foundations."[11] Dr. Eidsmoe points out that if we blame Columbus for all the bad things that happened to the Indians because of Europeans coming to America, then in fairness, we must also credit him for the good things.

The politically correct crowd tries to have it both ways. They want to blame Columbus and Christianity for all the bad things, but at the same time deprive them of any credit for the good things. Dr. Eidsmoe says of the Europeans and their descendants who settled North America:

> [L]et us credit them for its [Western culture's] achievements and contributions: art, music, architecture, ethics, liberty, law, government, a Constitution that has served as a model across the world, an economic system that has produced the greatest good for the greatest number and the highest level of prosperity the world has ever known, and a spirit of ingenuity and achievement that led to unparalleled medical and technological advances.[12]

> *"Faith liberated Columbus from the chains of human myopia, propelling him to the providential encounter with a vast territory and a multitude of peoples with their indigenous cultures up to that time unknown to Europeans."*
>
> Kay Brigham, Columbus translator and biographer in her 1991 translation of Columbus' *Book of Prophecies*

If we remove Christianity and its impact on Columbus, we must then remove the man entirely, because without his faith and his belief in God's call upon his life, it is unlikely he would ever have attempted to sail to the West.

We are not claiming that Columbus was a perfect saint. He certainly was a man of flesh and blood with feet of clay; and there is no doubt he did a poor job as governor of Hispaniola, the Caribbean island he ruled for a short time (the modern-day island of the Dominican Republic and Haiti). Columbus obviously lacked administrative skills, but it does not automatically follow that he was barbaric or cruel.

The barbaric acts of Spanish and Portuguese explorers who were only seeking riches and cared nothing for the indigenous populations cannot be used to indict the motives of Columbus, which included a desire to fulfill prophecy, to preach the Gospel, to reach the Indies, and to raise money for his ultimate goal – recapturing Jerusalem from the Muslims.

Harvard professor Samuel Huntington wrote, "When Westerners went out to conquer the world in the sixteenth century, they did so for God as well as gold."[13] This was certainly true for Christopher Columbus.

It was Europeans who discovered America; and it was European Christians who became the world's great explorers. The reason lies within Christianity itself, both in the Great Commission and in the great joy of the message. Those people who understand what God has done for them and what a glorious future He has in store for His people cannot help but tell others about Him. Spreading Christianity to the ends of the earth has been the task of the Church from the very beginning.

The origin of the United States of America is closely linked to spreading God's Kingdom and preaching the Gospel to those who need a Savior. Christopher Columbus and the Pilgrims came to America for the same reason: "To the glory of God and the advancement of the Christian faith" (The Mayflower Compact).

> "... our Redeemer has given this triumph to our most illustrious King and Queen, and to their renewed realms ... "
>
> Christopher Columbus,
> 1493 Letter to
> Ferdinand and Isabella

Before Columbus

Christopher Columbus was not the first known European to reach our continent. There is now solid and credible evidence that the man who deserves the honor of being first is the Norwegian Viking Leif Erickson (975-1020), who also came at least in part for "the glory of God."

Around the year 1000, Christianity began to take root among the Vikings of Norway and Denmark, and Leif Erickson followed his father Erik the Red to Greenland. The Viking lord, Olav Tryggvarson, was a convert to Christianity; and, according to the Norwegian "Saga" (early history), Olav sent the first priest to Greenland with Leif Erickson. Their mission was to establish a church in Greenland and to preach the Gospel of Christ to the native people. Leif Erickson's voyage took place around 1001-1002. He was blown off course and landed in what he called *Vinland det Gode*, his name for America, which meant "The Good Wineland." Most scholars believe that Leif went ashore in Nova Scotia and Newfoundland, where Viking settlements have been found. Even though the Norwegian seafarer did not set out to reach America (or Vinland), there is no doubt that the purpose for his voyage was to spread the Christian faith. Leif Erickson's discovery, however, did not lead to any lasting relationship between the old world and the new; and so the American continent remained unknown in Europe for another five hundred years. It was left for Columbus to discover the New World; and he became one of a handful of men about whom it can truly be said, they changed world history.

The Collapse of Byzantium

It is important to understand a calamity that occurred in the 15th century, when Columbus was just an infant. That calamity eventually helped motivate the man to prepare for his historic voyage. In 1453, the Ottoman Turks besieged the Christian city of Constantinople. The fate of Christians living there at the time was grim. George Grant writes:

> The great city had gone down fighting, with Emperor Constantine bravely at the head of his troops. But the fierce Moslem tide was too much. All Christian resistance was quickly thwarted. The conquest was complete by mid-morning. The massacre that followed was utterly horrifying – Byzantine citizens were cut down like grass in a meadow, holy relics were tossed profligately into the sea, diplomatic consuls from the West were tortured and executed, women were raped, children were enslaved, and the once magnificent city was reduced to ruin.[14]

> "... *Go ye into all the world, and preach the gospel to every creature.*"
>
> Mark 16:15

Thus, the Muslim invaders destroyed the Byzantine Empire, which had lasted for more than a millennium. It cannot be emphasized enough that the fall of the Byzantine Empire in 1453 set the stage for Columbus' voyage in 1492. The Muslims now had *complete* control over all known routes to the East, threatening all Christendom. All trade was effectively cut off between Europe and Asia.

Furthermore, the Muslims were not content merely with taking over Byzantium. They wanted to control all of Europe as well. Historian and law professor Dr. John Eidsmoe points out: "The Muslims looked upon Europe as a prize to be secured in the name of Allah."[15] The context of Columbus' historic voyage to America was the ongoing conflict between two competing forces: Christianity and Islam.

At that time, it was generally believed the earth was round, so the possibility of reaching Asia by going west seemed plausible. But was it merely the opening up of a new trade route that drew Columbus to the sea? He said himself that the Lord gave him the vision to do what he did. And he added, "No one should be afraid to take on any enterprise in the name of our Savior, if it is right and if the purpose is purely for his holy service."[16]

Like many Christians throughout the ages, Columbus believed he was living in the last days. He wrote in his *Book of Prophecies*:

> The Holy Scriptures testify in the Old Testament, by the mouth of the prophets, and in the New [Testament], by our Savior Jesus Christ, that this world will come to an end: Matthew, Mark, and Luke have recorded the signs of the end of the age. . . . And I say that the sign which convinces me that our Lord is hastening the end of the world is the preaching of the Gospel recently in so many lands.[17]

Columbus felt an urgency from the Lord, not merely to open a new trade route, but also to bring the Gospel to the ends of the earth. His purpose was twofold. First, of course, he wanted to reach Asia. Secondly, in the words of the *World Book Encyclopedia*, he wanted to use the proceeds from his expedition to "recapture Jerusalem from the Muslims. There, he said, he would rebuild the Jews' holy Temple and bring on a new 'Age of the Holy Spirit.'"[18] He wanted to liberate Christ's holy sepulcher from Muslim ownership back to Christian control. Because of all this, George Grant calls him "the last crusader."

> *"To Columbus, the voyage westward was a way of reaching the Orient, and after Christianizing the Orient, joining forces with Asia to turn back the threat of Islam."*
>
> John Eidsmoe,
> *Columbus & Cortez*

A Praying Man or a Preying Man?

Columbus is described by biographer and Columbus-translator Kay Brigham as a man of prayer and a devoted Christian. She points out that it was his "unquenchable faith in divine Providence which enabled him to achieve in the face of adversities and hardships."[19] Overall, he had a kindly attitude toward the natives and was concerned about their salvation. But this is not the picture of him presented today.

My co-author Jerry Newcombe has told me how his own children were part of a field trip to the Broward Center for the Performing Arts in Fort Lauderdale, Florida, to see a play about Christopher Columbus. In it, Columbus was portrayed as a greedy exploiter of the natives. His only motive was wealth, and all his ways were depicted as cruel and barbaric. Instead of bringing the Gospel, he was accused of bringing disease and violence to a peaceful people. But listen to Columbus' own words in a letter to the King and Queen of Spain, written on February 15, 1493, during his return voyage:

> I forbade that they [the Indians] should be given things so worthless as pieces of broken crockery and broken glass, and lace points. . . . I gave them a thousand good, pleasing things which I had bought, in order that they might be fond of us, and furthermore might become Christians and be inclined to the love and service of Their Highnesses and of the whole Castilian nation [Spain], and try to help us and to give us of the things which they have in abundance and which are necessary to us.[20]

> *"Columbus' use of the Bible is one of the best documented facts of his remarkable career, but it is one of the least known to the general public."*
>
> August J. Kling,
> *Moody Monthly,*
> October 1972

In short, Columbus tried to implement Christ's golden rule in his initial dealings with Native Americans. But we would never know that today. The modern anti-Columbus performance in Ft. Lauderdale is typical of today's secular revisionist attitude, one which at its heart is anti-Western Civilization and at its core is really anti-Christian.

A Study in Perseverance

Columbus was one of the most determined men who ever lived. It took him a long time to convince his superiors to finance his eventful voyage. Historian George Bancroft says he spent "ten years of vain solicitations in Portugal."[21] Then it took him several more years to convince King Ferdinand and Queen Isabella of Spain to finance his journey. But he never lost faith in his mission.

Even his Christian name, Christopher, means "Christ-bearer." It refers to a legend in which the original St. Christopher carried the Christ Child across a stream. Columbus himself tells of the Christian motivation for his voyage in his *Book of Prophecies*, a volume he wrote in 1505, so named because he quotes many Biblical prophecies:

> It was the Lord who put into my mind (I could feel His hand upon me) to sail to the Indies. All who heard of my project rejected it with laughter, ridiculing me. There is no question that the inspiration was from the Holy Spirit, because He comforted me with rays of marvelous illumination from the Holy Scriptures.[22]

Columbus elaborates further:

For the execution of the journey to the Indies I did not make use of intelligence,
mathematics, or maps. It is simply the fulfillment of what Isaiah prophesied. . .
These are great and wonderful things for the earth, and the signs are that the
Lord is hastening the end. The fact that [the] gospel must still be preached to
so many lands in such a short time – this is what convinces me.[23]

Until the end of his life, Columbus "steadfastly believed" that he had
discovered "the outposts of India."[24] To this day, the term "Indians" that he coined
is still the general name applied to Native Americans.

Blessed Be. . . the Holy Trinity

When Columbus and his men left the Canary
Islands on August 12, 1492, it would be two long
months before they finally spotted land in what is
now known as the Bahamas. After seventy-one days
on the ocean, it was little wonder some in his crew
mumbled threats of mutiny. In his diary, Columbus
often repeated this refrain, "And this day we sailed
on."

> *"If he had known that the distance was really 12,000 miles, perhaps he would never have set sail; certainly his crew wouldn't have gone."*
>
> Desmond Wilcox,
> *Ten Who Dared*

On that fateful morning of October 12, 1492,
Columbus ran off the *Santa Maria* (named for the mother of our Lord) weeping
for joy. Then he looked up to God and proclaimed the words of the morning
prayer he and his crew had been praying every day on their long voyage:

> Blessed be the light of day
> And the Holy Cross, we say;
> And the Lord of Verity
> And the Holy Trinity.
> Blessed be th' immortal soul
> And the Lord who keeps it whole
> Blessed be the light of day
> And He who sends the night away.[25]

Columbus erected a cross on the landing site, symbolizing the claim of
Christ on a land that had not previously been exposed to the Gospel. He named
the first island on which they landed "San Salvador," which translated means

"Holy Savior." Other lands he later named included "Trinidad" (meaning "Trinity"), "Vera Cruz" (meaning "True Cross"), and "Navidad" (similar to our word "Nativity," meaning Christmas). These Christian names remain to this day.

Conclusion

We must continue to remember the great contributions Christopher Columbus made to Western Civilization. We must join Columbus in giving "thanks to our Lord and Saviour Jesus Christ, who has bestowed upon us so great a victory and gift."[26] We should remember every Columbus Day holiday to celebrate the salvation of countless souls throughout the centuries in America, made possible by his voyage. And may we never forget America's dependence on God.

So we have seen that the first thing every Christian should know about the founding of America is that Christopher Columbus changed history by his voyage, a voyage that was ultimately motivated by his Christian faith. Next, we will look at a whole group of settlers, beginning with the Pilgrims, whose devotion to Christ is well known by all, even the ungodly.

Chapter 2
The Mayflower Compact

"Dearly beloved, I beseech you as strangers and pilgrims . . ."
~ 1 Peter 2:11

The Pilgrims clearly stated that they came to the New World to glorify God and to advance the Christian faith.

I n a very real way, America began "in the name of God. Amen." Those were the first words of our nation's first self-governing document, the Mayflower Compact, which became the cornerstone of our present Constitution and of our republic. The second thing every Christian should know about the founding of America is that the Pilgrims clearly stated that they came to the New World to glorify God and to advance the Christian faith.

It All Began With a Covenant

Most students are familiar with the fact that the Pilgrims came to America in 1620 seeking religious liberty and landed at Plymouth Rock. What most students probably do not know is that when these Godly adventurers were blown off course while heading for the "Virginia" colony, they were given a divine opportunity to create a written covenant to govern themselves. The Pilgrims chose to make this written covenant, the Mayflower Compact, a political version of their congregation's original spiritual covenant.

Paul Jehle is an expert on Pilgrim history. He serves as Director of Education for the Plymouth Rock Foundation, an organization based in Plymouth, Massachusetts, "America's Home Town." Jehle is dedicated to the rediscovery of America's Christian heritage. He leads tours in Plymouth and trains young students in his Christian school for the same purpose – to understand the Christian roots of America.

Jehle describes how this separatist congregation of Pilgrims meeting secretly in Scrooby, England formed at the beginning of the 17th century – they made a covenant with God and with each other. He says of this bond:

It was a covenant [in which] they all agreed to have their lives exposed one to another, whatever it should cost them, if they were going to walk in "unity and purity of the gospel," as Bradford would have phrased it. And this Scrooby congregation got its identity at that time.[1]

> "The more they studied the New Testament, the less they could find bearing a resemblance to that or any other National Church."
>
> Leonard Bacon,
> Genesis of the
> New England Churches, 1874

Our main source of information about the Pilgrims comes from the writings of William Bradford (1590-1656), who served as the elected governor of the Plymouth colony for more than thirty years. Bradford penned one of the first great books ever written in America, *Of Plymouth Plantation*, in which he tells his firsthand story of how the Pilgrims began what unquestionably became *the* most important settlement in the New World. Governor Bradford had joined this covenant group as a young man, despite the severe disapproval of his uncles who were rearing him. He remained closely associated with the Pilgrim community until he died.

Cotton Mather, Puritan pastor, author of *The Great Works of Christ in America*, saw the Pilgrim experience as a continuation, a fulfillment, of what the Reformation had begun a hundred years earlier:

A number of devout and serious Christians in the English nation, finding the Reformation of the Church in that nation, according to the Word of God, and the design of many among the first Reformers . . . they did, Anno 1602, in the north of England, enter into a covenant, wherein expressing themselves desirous, not only to attend the *worship* of our Lord Jesus Christ, with a freedom from [human] *inventions* and *additions*, but also to enjoy all the

Evangelical Institutions of that worship, they did like those Macedonians, that are *therefore* by the Apostle Paul commended, "give themselves up, first unto God, and then to one another." These pious people [found] that their brethren and neighbours in the Church of England, as then *established by law*, took offence at these their endeavours after a *scriptural reformation*.[2]

Rev. John Robinson

The Pilgrims were Bible-believers who refused to conform to the heretical state Church of England. Their movement was outlawed; and their secret congregational meetings in Scrooby, England, were held in the manor home of William Brewster (1567-1644), who remained a key leader of the Pilgrim community as that group emigrated first to Holland and later to America.

The Reverend John Robinson (c. 1575-1625) became the chief minister of the Scrooby congregation. He remained their pastor when the group moved to Leyden, Holland, to escape persecution in England. In 1620, the Pilgrims decided to immigrate to America in order to protect their children from the ungodly influences that were drawing them away from the faith in the more secularized culture of Holland.

> *Rev. John Robinson is "the father of the Independents."*
>
> Daniel Neal,
> *History of the Puritans,* 1731

Rev. Robinson never made that voyage to America himself. It was widely believed that the pastor would be of more profit to the remnant group that stayed behind in Holland while the initial adventurers sailed to the New World. So Rev. Robinson shepherded the group that stayed behind in Europe, constantly seeking ways to send more of their number to America as soon as it was feasible.

Although Rev. Robinson did not participate in the historic *Mayflower* voyage, he instructed his flock well before they left. He encouraged the immigrants to live out the Reformation and to seek more treasures from God's Word. Cotton Mather tells about a moving farewell scene on board the ship: "Their excellent pastor, on his knees, by the *sea-side*, poured out their mutual petitions unto God; and having wept in one another's arms, as long as the *wind* and the *tide* would permit them, they bad[e] *adieu*."[3]

Edward Winslow (1595-1655), one of the Pilgrims about to sail for America, said of Robinson's farewell message: "Here also he put us in mind of our church covenant, at least that part of it whereby we promise and covenant with God and one another to receive whatsoever light or truth shall be made known to us from his written Word."[4]

Rev. Robinson also exhorted the travelers by sending along a letter of instruction and encouragement for them. He reminded them to continue the pattern of self-government they had been following as a congregation for years. Here was the beginning of democracy in action in America:

> Lastly, whereas you are to become a body politic, using amongst yourselves civil government, and are not furnished with any persons of special eminence above the rest, to be chosen by you into office of government. Let your wisdom and godliness appear, not only in choosing such persons as do entirely love, and will diligently promote the common good, but also in yielding unto them all due honor and obedience in their lawful administrations.[5]

The Pilgrims were instructed to live out their covenant by walking with God and living in good fellowship with one another. Cotton Mather tells us:

> [T]he faithful pastor [John Robinson] of this people immediately sent after them a *pastoral letter*, a letter filled with holy counsels unto them, to settle their *peace* with God in their own consciences, by an exact *repentance* of all sin whatsoever, that so they might more easily bear all the difficulties that were now before them; and then to maintain a good *peace* with one another, and beware of giving or taking *offences*.[6]

> *"It was resolved, that part of the Church should go [to America] before their brethren, to prepare a place for the rest; and whereas the minor part of younger and stronger men were to go first, the Pastor was to stay with the major, till they should see cause to follow."*
>
> Cotton Mather,
> *The Great Works of Christ in America*, Volume I

In the rotunda of the U. S. Capitol, our nation's spiritual heritage is honored even today among eight large paintings depicting important moments in American history. About half of these paintings have a direct reference in one way or another to Christ, including the Christian baptism of Pocahontas.

One of these paintings depicts Rev. Robinson's prayer meeting with the Pilgrims on board ship before they departed for America. In the picture, Robinson is holding a large open Bible. The name of Jesus Christ can clearly be seen (upside down) on the open page of the Scriptures. Visitors to Washington, D.C., can visit this very large historic painting. The picture stands as a beacon of our nation's true history.

While Pastor John Robinson had every intention of later going to Plymouth, he died in 1625 before he could fulfill that dream. When Rev. Robinson passed away, many Christians of different denominations affirmed "[t]hat all the Churches of our Lord Jesus Christ had sustained a great loss by the death of this worthy man."[7]

Stepping Stones

Why did some of the Pilgrims choose to travel to the New World, even though the voyage would be difficult and they might never see their friends again? William Bradford later explained the reason for their immigration. Of the Pilgrims, he wrote:

> [A] great hope and inward zeal they had of laying some good foundation, or
> at least to make some way thereunto, for the propagating and advancing the
> gospel of the kingdom of Christ in those remote parts of the world; yea,
> though they should be but even as stepping-stones unto others for the
> performing of so great a work.[8]

The goal of the Pilgrims was to experience religious freedom for themselves and for those who would follow after them, and to apply the Bible as the basis for their community life. The Gospel was at the heart of everything they were doing.

Under No Government's Jurisdiction

The Pilgrims had intended to sail to the Hudson Bay area, which was then part of the Virginia colony, but they were blown off course. For several days in November 1620, they explored the Cape Cod coastline looking for a place to settle. When they discovered they were not in Virginia and, therefore, technically not under any governmental jurisdiction, some of the "strangers" (non-Pilgrims) among the group began whispering about the possibility of striking out on their own. That would have been disastrous for everybody. The Pilgrims had carefully chosen each man, including the "strangers" among them, for his unique skills. Each was absolutely necessary for the survival of the colony. So the Pilgrims did something unprecedented. They decided to draft a governing document for themselves – a decision that would change the course of history.

Since the Pilgrims had begun their congregation by a covenant (albeit a spiritual one), they now decided to govern themselves in a similar manner. A written charter was agreed upon, binding them as a group before God and to each other. Aboard the ship, before any man disembarked, they each bound themselves to a political covenant that essentially echoed their congregation's spiritual covenant.

If the Pilgrims ever wrote down their initial spiritual covenant of 1606, it has not survived. But copies of their *civil* covenant, which committed the entire colony to God and to each other for the good and preservation of them all, did survive. This agreement for self-government, the Mayflower Compact, was signed November 11, 1620. It became the cornerstone of the U. S. Constitution. The Mayflower Compact begins by recognizing the hand of God who had been leading them all along:

> *"What was remarkable about this particular contract [the Mayflower Compact] was that it was not between a servant and a master, or a people and a king, but between a group of like-minded individuals and each other, with God as a witness and symbolic co-signatory."*
>
> Paul Johnson,
> *A History of the American People*

In the name of God, Amen. We, whose names are underwritten, the Loyal Subjects of our dread Sovereign Lord, King *James* . . . Having undertaken for the Glory of God, and Advancement of the Christian Faith, and the Honour of our King and Country, a voyage to plant the first colony in the northern Parts of Virginia; do by these Presents, solemnly and mutually in the Presence of God and one of another, covenant and combine ourselves together into a civil Body Politick, for our better Ordering and Preservation, and Furtherance of the Ends aforesaid . . . [9]

The significance of the Mayflower Compact cannot be over-emphasized. Here was a group of travel-weary, Godly men and women, blown off course in their voyage – and thus technically under no governmental supervision – creating their own government. They agreed before God, through the instrument of the Mayflower Compact, to "covenant and combine" themselves together into a "Body Politick."

Historian Paul Johnson, author of *A History of the American People*, relates the obvious source of the Pilgrims' foundational idea to make such a binding agreement with each other. It was the Bible. Speaking of the Mayflower Compact, this eminent historian writes: "This contract was based upon the original Biblical covenant between God and the Israelites."[10] Johnson points out the lasting importance of this document:

> It is an amazing document. . . . What was remarkable about this particular contract was that it was not between a servant and a master, or a people and a king, but between a group of like-minded individuals and each other, with God as a witness and symbolic co-signatory.[11]

• Where did the Pilgrims believe their liberties came from? They came from God, Who they believed had ordained the whole venture.

• Why did the Pilgrims choose to come to the New World? They said it was for the advancement of the Christian faith.

• Where did the Pilgrims believe their political power came from? From the people, they said.

• From where did they believe any ruler among them would derive his power? From the people, under God.

The Mayflower Compact contained every one of these seeds from which both the Declaration of Independence and the United States Constitution would flower.

The Declaration of Independence, drafted by Thomas Jefferson over a hundred years after the Mayflower Compact was signed, referred to the events surrounding the origins of the colonies in his list of grievances against the King: "We have reminded them [our British Brethren] of the Circumstances of our Emigration and Settlement here."[12] Did Thomas Jefferson and the others who signed the Declaration of Independence have the Pilgrims in mind? Probably so, as well as all the other immigrants, a great many of whom came to the New World seeking religious freedom.

While adventurers came to the New World for a number of reasons, including commerce, American self-government began in a very large measure because of the desire of these religious dissidents to seek religious freedom and to base their civic lives together on the laws of God. This knowledge of the true history of America is what makes the current revisionist mindset of many Americans so disturbing. At the Christian Law Association, we see over and over again that the rights of religious people are being trumped in modern America. This attitude is totally foreign to what the founding spirit of America was all about. It seems we have forgotten our history.

The late Dr. Robert Bartlett, author and direct Pilgrim descendant, points out:

The Mayflower Compact was the first great American document both religious and political. The first agreement among a group of people who formed their own government; and it was signed before they landed in Plymouth because they wanted to come ashore with some purpose that might hold them together and give them direction.[13]

Conclusion

Peter Marshall, co-author of the classic book, *The Light and the Glory*, makes a striking observation: "This was the only place on the face of the earth where free Christian people were creating their own government, electing their own civil leadership – the only time in history, as a matter of fact, when a nation, from scratch, was based on God's Word."[14]

And so we see that the second thing every Christian should know about the founding of America is that it all began "in the name of God. Amen."

Chapter 3
The Puritan Covenants

"And I will make my covenant between me and thee,
and will multiply thee exceedingly."
~ Genesis 17:2

The Puritans created Bible-based commonwealths
in order to practice a representative government
that was modeled on their church covenants.

The idea of covenant is central to the modern American political system. This is no accident. The Founding Fathers did not sit down and invent a covenant form of government when they assembled to write a constitution for their new nation. Instead, they drew from a tradition that had been in existence for a century and a half, beginning with the Mayflower Compact and continuing with a number of even more highly developed Puritan covenants.

The third thing every Christian should know about the founding of America is that the Puritans, who followed the Pilgrims to New England, created Bible-based commonwealths in order to practice a representative government that was modeled on their church covenants. Their more than one hundred governmental covenants and compacts essentially laid the foundation for America's Constitution, which was drafted in 1787 and ratified in 1789.

Pilgrims vs. Puritans

Sometimes people think there was no difference between the Pilgrims and the Puritans. It is correct that both the Pilgrims and Puritans were dissenting English Protestants; so in that sense, we could say (and some have said) that the Pilgrims were merely a subset of the Puritans. But it gives a more accurate picture to make a complete distinction between the two groups.

Both the Pilgrims and Puritans disagreed with many things about the Church of England in their day. But the Pilgrims felt that reforming the church was a hopeless endeavor. They were led to separate themselves from the official church and to hold their worship services in a completely different manner. Hence, they were often labeled "Separatists."

> *"The Puritan searched the Bible, not only for principles and rules, but for mandates, – and, when he could find none of these, for analogies, – to guide him in precise arrangements of public administration, and in the minutest points of individual conduct."*
>
> John Palfrey,
> *History of New England,* 1859

The Puritans, on the other hand, wanted to reform the Church of England from within. They were not convinced this would be an impossible task. They argued from within for the purity of the church. Hence, the name Puritans.

The Pilgrims paved the way for other Protestant nonconformists to come to these shores. The Puritans did not initially join them; but nearly a decade later, the king granted them a charter and several groups of Puritans also set sail for the New World. By this time, the Pilgrims had gained a toehold in the New World, and the Puritans determined it would be a good place to develop their concept of a Bible commonwealth.

These Puritan men and women were not refugees in the commonly understood sense of that word. They were not "tired, poor, and huddled masses" of immigrants. Instead, these Puritans were well-educated, wealthy, smart, professional men, traveling with their families. The Church of England was actually driving away its best and brightest. England's spiritual loss was America's gain.

Salem – The First Major Puritan Settlement

King Charles I allowed the Puritans to leave England and granted them the charter they needed to establish the Massachusetts Bay colony. Cotton Mather tells us: "By this Charter they were empowered yearly to elect their own governour, deputy-governour and magistrates; as also to make such laws as they should think suitable for the plantation."[1] Thus, following the lead of the Pilgrims, the first major Puritan settlement in the New World also began with self-government.

Soon after the first Puritans arrived in Salem they called for a day of fasting and prayer in August 1629. Their goal, according to Cotton Mather's early history of New England, was to settle "a *Church State* among them, and for making a *Confession of their Faith*, and entering into an holy *Covenant*, whereby that Church State was formed."[2] It is important to remember that the Puritan colonies were Bible commonwealths where Scripture was the center of community life. Their initial covenant, while religious in nature, also identified itself as politically binding:

We covenant with our Lord, and one with another; and we do bind our selves in the presence of God, to walk together in all his ways, according as he is pleased to reveal himself unto us in his blessed word of truth; and do explicitly, in the name and fear of God, profess and protest to walk as followeth, through the power and grace of our Lord Jesus Christ.[3]

> "... *wherever they sat down, they were so mindful of their errand into the wilderness, that still one of their first works was to gather a church into the covenant and order of the gospel.*"
>
> Cotton Mather,
> The Great Works of
> Christ in America,
> Volume I

The rest of the covenant continued in a similar manner. The Puritans agreed to get along with each other and to live out the Gospel in peace, harmony, and justice. Just as the Pilgrims had drafted their own covenant to form a "civil Body Politick," it was the practice of religious nonconformists all over New England, including the Puritans, to form a political covenant – committing themselves to God first and then to each other. This practice, which was common in New England, ultimately paved the way for the United States Constitution, which governs us to this day.

Church and State

When our Constitution and Bill of Rights went into effect in 1789, America was a united federation of states, some of which were still governing themselves according to their own unique religious beliefs. Although official state religions had long since fallen out of favor by the 20th century, it was not until 1947 that the United States Supreme Court made it unconstitutional for state and local governments to choose to govern themselves according to the religious dictates of their citizens. However, because state and local governments were permitted to have their own unique religious beliefs prior to 1947, it was not considered unconstitutional for local governments to determine, for instance, what prayers should be said in their public schools and what religious observances would dominate their civic institutions.

The 1947 decision in the case of *Everson vs. Board of Education* was the first time the United States Supreme Court applied the restrictions of the Establishment Clause of the First Amendment ("Congress shall make no law respecting an establishment of religion") to state and local governments as well as to the federal government. This 1947 decision was also the first time the Supreme Court applied the concept of "the separation of church and state" to Establishment Clause jurisprudence.

> *"In a sense, the clergy were the first elected officials of the new American society, a society which to that extent had a democratic element from the start . . . "*
>
> Paul Johnson,
> *A History of the American People*

The First Colonial Election

The first American use of ballots for an election occurred in Salem. The issue? Choosing a minister and choosing a Christian teacher. George Bancroft, an early historian, points out: "Such is the origin of the use of the ballot on this continent; [Samuel] Skelton was chosen pastor and [Francis] Higginson teacher."[4]

John Winthrop's Famous Speech

John Winthrop was the leader of another group of Puritans who came to America in 1630. He gave a classic speech, known as "A Model of Christian Charity," while on board their ship, the *Arbella*, In the course of this lengthy exhortation, he called on the settlers to make Christian love the hallmark of their new colony. He recalled to their minds the main idea of covenant: "Thus stands the cause between God and us. We are entered into covenant with Him for this work."[5] Winthrop further elaborated:

> Now if the Lord shall please to hear us, and bring us in peace to the place we desire, then He has ratified this covenant and sealed our commission, and will expect a strict performance of the articles contained in it. But if we neglect to

observe these articles, which are the ends we have propounded, and – dissembling with our God – shall embrace this present world and prosecute our carnal intentions, seeking great things for ourselves and our posterity, the Lord will surely break out in wrath against us and be revenged of such a perjured people, and He will make us know the price of the breach of such a covenant.[6]

This Biblical idea of covenant was very significant. Winthrop was explaining that the Puritans had made a covenant with God to obey Him in the wilderness. Their government and civic responsibilities were not simply laws agreed upon by the governed. Instead, their solemn covenant was with the Lord – to obey Him.

What were the standards the Puritans were expected to follow? The answer is found in Micah 6:8. Winthrop continued:

> Now the only way to avoid this shipwreck and to provide for our posterity is to follow the counsel of Micah: to do justly, to love mercy, to walk humbly with our God. For this end, we must be knit together in this work as one man.[7]

".... New England religion was so powerful a force in people's lives and of such direct and continuing assistance in building a new society from nothing."

Paul Johnson,
A History of the American People

The Written Page

What central idea governs America today? At least theoretically, it is the Constitution, our nation's written and signed agreement for self-government. But it is important to realize that there is a direct link between the Bible and our modern Constitution, a link initiated by the Pilgrims and developed more fully by the Puritans.

There had been no written Constitution in England. The British common law was a mostly oral tradition, articulated as necessary in various written court decisions. However, since the Puritans had carefully studied the Bible and had made it the center of their colonial life together, they determined to anchor their liberties on the written page, a tradition taken from the Bible.

Our present Constitution is not merely an outgrowth of the church covenants written by the Puritans, although it is certainly that. But the concept of a written political constitution is also an outgrowth of the Protestant practice of making the written page central to civil government, following the practice found in the Old Testament. Thus, the Puritans were indispensable mediators of the American constitutional experience.

Historian Clarence Carson comments in *The Colonial Experience: 1607-1774*:

> Since Christianity is a religion of the book, the written word assumes a special importance for Christians. Learning assumes a special importance. Careful construction of the meaning of words assumes a special importance. The original meaning, the original documents, the earliest applications, all assume a special importance. This is so especially for the scriptures, but the attitude and belief tend to be extended to more worldly books, documents, and words as well. While this attitude is true for all Christians, it is even stronger for Protestants than for others, and they set the religious tone for the United States.[8]

> *"It is written . . ."*
>
> Common phrase of the New Testament

The *written* Word of God ruled supreme in New England, especially for the Puritans. As Cotton Mather put it:

> New England was a wilderness planted by a people generally so remarkable in their holy zeal for the ordinances belonging to the house of God, that, for the sake of enjoying the administrations of those ordinances with *scriptural purity*, they had undergone the severe persecutions which at last exiled them into that American wilderness.[9]

The first time a code of laws was written down in New England was December 1641 when the Puritans commissioned the services of Rev. Nathaniel Ward of Ipswich, a minister who also had some legal training. Rev. Ward created the Massachusetts Body of Liberties, which, like just about everything else in Puritan New England, was based on the Bible.

This Body of Liberties was premised on the belief that Christ's rule is not only given for the church, but also for the state. It contained principles found in the Bible, specifically "ninety-eight separate protections of individual rights, including: 'no taxation without representation,' 'due process of law,' 'trial by a jury of peers,' and prohibitions against 'cruel and unusual punishment.'"[10] Indeed, the Bible was central to the Puritan commonwealth, and the Puritan commonwealth helped set the framework for the laws and liberties we now enjoy in the United States of America.

The Synod of 1648

The Puritans were constantly considering and formulating their views on issues of church and government. They drafted numerous legal codes of conduct, codes of liberties, and guidelines for civil liberty. Again, the Bible was the basis for them all.

The Bible did not merely govern their *spiritual* lives. It also formed the basis for their *political* views. For example, the Puritan divines of New England held a synod in Cambridge, Massachusetts on September 30, 1648, in which they drafted a Platform of Church-discipline known as *Synodicon Americanum*, "the American Church Manual." In this manual, they articulated their thoroughly Christian beliefs on virtually every subject imaginable, including the Gospel, religious worship, and marriage. In "Chapter XXIV. Of the Civil Magistrate," they wrote:

> *"God alone is Lord of the conscience . . . "*
>
> Chapter XXI of "The American Church Manual," written September 30, 1648

God, the supreme Lord and King of all the world, hath ordained civil magistrates to be under him, over the people for his own glory and the public good: And to this end has armed them with the power of the sword for the defence and encouragement of them that do good, and for the punishment of evil doers.[11]

The ultimate source of political power, as the Puritans saw it, was God Himself. Human rulers must rule under His dominion:

It is lawful for Christians to accept and execute the office of a magistrate, when called thereunto: In the management whereof, as they ought especially to maintain piety, justice and peace, according to the wholesome laws of each common-wealth, so for that end, they may lawfully now under the New Testament wage war upon just and necessary occasion.[12]

The Puritans did not view politics as a dirty business, as has sometimes been the case for modern Christians. For them, politics was a Biblical undertaking.

The Responsibility of the People

The Puritans continued to develop their views on government, views which came directly out of a theocratic framework. They were trying to create a new

Israel, a new theocracy where God was the ruler through the ministrations of elected magistrates.

Within this same theological context, the Puritans also set forth in their "American Church Manual" the responsibilities of the people, including the clergy, toward their rulers:

> It is the duty of people to pray for magistrates, to honour their persons, to pay them tribute and other dues, to obey their lawful commands, and to be subject to their authority for conscience sake. Infidelity or difference in religion does not make void the magistrate's just and legal authority, nor free the people from their due obedience to him: . . . [E]cclesiastical persons are not exempted.[13]

> *The Bible "was the professed, perpetual and only directory [guide] of these churches . . . "*
>
> Cotton Mather on the churches of New England

The Puritan Congregationalist ministers – and they were all Congregationalists then – met in Cambridge, Massachusetts, to draft these law codes within two decades of the Puritans' arrival in the New World. The codes were written down for the purpose of articulating their governing principles, including their principles of civil government. What was their central guide and authority? It was the Word of God, said Cotton Mather.[14]

Since the Puritans believed the Bible, they knew well what Scripture teaches about the sinfulness of man. So they created a system of government that did not permit too much power to flow into the hands of any one person or group. Mather states: "[T]here is a dispersion of powers into several hands."[15]

More than a century later, the Founding Fathers who framed the American Constitution would apply this very same principle. However, it would not necessarily be correct to say that James Madison and the other founders who drafted our federal Constitution, with its separation of powers, took the idea of man's sinfulness from the Puritans. It would be more accurate to say that for both the Puritans and the Founding Fathers, the Bible was the ultimate source for their view of the nature of man.

The First Complete Constitution

Despite the fact that our modern Constitution was drafted in Philadelphia, the motor vehicle license plates of Connecticut identify that state as "the Constitution State." Why would the State of Connecticut make this claim for itself? The answer is because the Puritan founders of Connecticut really did write the first complete colonial constitution in America – and, yes, it too was a spiritual/political *covenant.*

Can you imagine a colony being founded and its constitution being framed on the basis of *a sermon?* That is exactly what happened in Connecticut. John Fiske, in his 1889 work, *Beginnings of New England,* related that the Fundamental Orders of Connecticut, a document drafted in 1639, was inspired by a 1638 sermon preached by the Rev. Thomas Hooker, founder of the colony. Fiske reported:

> [He] preached a sermon of wonderful power, in which he maintained that "the foundation of authority is laid in the free consent of the people, that the choice of public magistrates belongs unto the people by God's own allowance," and that "they who have power to appoint officers and magistrates have the right also to set the bounds and limitations of the power and place unto which they call them."[16]

In 1884, George Leon Walker, in his monograph, "History of the First Church in Hartford - 1633-1883," said that the Fundamental Orders of Connecticut has been called "the first written constitution . . . in the history of nations."[17] Three years before the drafting of the Fundamental Orders of Connecticut, the Pilgrims had already drafted the Pilgrim Code of Law of 1636. The Pilgrim Code of Law, however, was not as complete a document or as well known as the Fundamental Orders.

John Fiske believed that the Fundamental Orders of Connecticut "marked the beginnings of American democracy, of which Thomas Hooker deserves more than any other man to be called the father."[18] Fiske also offers this opinion: "The government of the United States today is in lineal descent more nearly related to that of Connecticut than to that of any of the other thirteen colonies."[19] All the various Pilgrim and Puritan covenants and law codes have paved the way to *the* present American Constitution, and all of these self-governing documents were entirely theologically based. But only Connecticut can claim the honor on its license tags of being the first state to actually develop a state constitution to govern themselves, rather than just a covenant or law code.

The New England Townhouse
The little white townhouses of Puritan New England were the cradle of our

representative government in so many ways. Like their churches where the people worshiped Christ on Sunday, these townhouses were always centrally located; and they were a perpetual reminder of the hallmark of New England: self-rule. In 1890, in his book, *Civil Government in the United States,* John Fiske declared the colonists' intent in centrally locating both their churches and their townhouses:

> All had for many generations been more or less accustomed to self-government and to public meetings for discussing local affairs. That self-government, especially as far as church matters were concerned, they were stoutly bent upon maintaining and extending. Indeed, that was what they had crossed the ocean for.[20]

> *"Never was any planta-tion [New England at large] brought unto such a considerableness, in a space of time so incon-siderable! an* howling wilderness *in a few* years became a pleasant land, *accommodated with the* necessaries — yea, and the conven-iences *of humane life;* the gospel *has carried with it a* fulness of all other blessings . . . "
>
> Cotton Mather

New England and Virginia

The colonies of New England were essentially a whole series of townships, where the people ruled themselves. Thomas Jefferson, the Virginian, looked in envy at this New England institution:

> Those wards, called townships in New England, are the vital principle of their governments, and have proved themselves the wisest invention ever devised by the wit of man for the perfect exercise of self-government, and for its preservation.[21]

Richard Frothingham was struck with the differences between New England and Virginia between 1680 and 1690. He draws this comparison in his 1890 book, *The Rise of the Republic:*

It was written of Virginia, that, "as it came out of the hands of God, it was certainly one of the best   countries in the world;" but as it respected well-built towns, well-educated children, and an industrious and thriving people, it was certainly "one of the poorest, miserablest, and worst countries in all America that was inhabited by Christians."[22]

While Virginia had greater natural resources than New England, the latter region actually prospered more than the former. Jamestown and similar southern colonies had been outwardly Christian, but the New England colonies were generally recognized as being both inwardly and outwardly Christian. It should be remembered that Virginia was a slave colony virtually from its very inception while slavery was less common in New England, and the abolitionist movement actually began in New England among the Christian community.

New England was industrious and prosperous. That was certainly not the case with Virginia where slaves did much of the labor. In her book, *Miracle at Philadelphia*, Catherine Drinker Bowen tells the story of some Frenchmen who visited America around the time the Constitution was written in 1787. They began their tour in the north and found these northern parts to be generally well-to-do. As they continued southward, they came across no poverty until they arrived in Virginia; and then conditions were generally worse.[23] It appears that the closer Americans followed the Puritan work ethic, the more prosperous they became.

Conclusion

Without a doubt, the Puritans helped shape the future course of the American nation. It was both their theological and political practices, as well as their written agreements for self-government based on the Bible, that have had the greatest impact on America. So, the third thing every Christian should know about the founding of America is that the Puritan practice of church covenants gave rise to the concept of political covenants, compacts, and written constitutions. Ultimately, these documents did much to inspire the United States Constitution, which survives to this day.

Chapter 4
A Haven for Religious Dissidents

*"Stand fast therefore in the liberty wherewith Christ hath made us free,
and be not entangled again with the yoke of bondage."*
~ Galatians 5:1

This nation was founded as a sanctuary for religious dissidents.

A merica began as a haven for Christian refugees – not only for the Pilgrims and Puritans who created colonies in New England; but also for the Huguenots, Presbyterians, Roman Catholics, Quakers, Baptists, German Dunkers, and many others. Many religious refugees still come to our shores today. Our Christian nation welcomes refugees of every faith, precisely because of its Biblical heritage, which mandates that every person must come to God without coercion and through a personal act of faith.

The fourth thing every Christian should know about the founding of America is that this nation was in large measure founded as a sanctuary for religious dissidents. In this chapter, we will turn from our study of the Pilgrims and Puritans and focus our attention on Roger Williams, who founded Rhode Island as a haven for religious nonconformists, and on William Penn, the Quaker who founded Pennsylvania. Finally, we will take a quick look at some other Christian nonconformists who were driven out of their own lands or who left of their own accord in order to gain greater religious liberty in colonial America.

Roger Williams

Wherever the story of freedom is told, Roger Williams (1603-1683), the founder of Rhode Island, must be remembered. He was a pioneer for Christian liberty. There are several large statues honoring the Protestant Reformation in a public park in Geneva, Switzerland. The largest include John Calvin and John Knox. To the left and right of these are about a dozen smaller statues commemorating other great Reformers. One of them is a statue honoring the memory of Roger Williams.

Roger Williams is sometimes represented in American history textbooks as a liberal who rejected Puritan doctrine. Some secularists attempt to present him today as a virtual unbeliever, but that image is totally false. Williams was a man completely shaped by his faith in Jesus Christ. Rhode Island, the legacy of freedom he created, was a product of Puritanism. But it was Roger Williams' own dissident Biblical views that got him into trouble with Puritan authorities, making it necessary for him to flee from Massachusetts and found Rhode Island as a haven for religious freedom.

> *John Winthrop was "the first great American." Roger Williams "was the second great American to emerge."*
>
> Historian Paul Johnson

If Puritanism means being strict about what you believe, then Roger Williams out-Puritaned the Puritans. While some in the Puritan colonies saw Williams as merely a contrarian – disagreeing just for the sake of disagreeing – God used him to help bring about a higher level of freedom in the United States.

Williams was one of those rare people for whom conviction is everything. Such people will live out their consciences, regardless of the consequences. Roger Williams did not set out to found a new colony; but he fell out of favor with both Puritan and Pilgrim leaders because of his strong reactions to viewpoints with which he could not agree. In the providence of God, Rhode Island became a new colony dedicated to religious freedom because its founder was a gifted man with strong Biblical principles and convictions.

What Williams Believed

One might say that Roger Williams and Gov. John Winthrop became "good enemies." They respected and helped each other, even as they argued over practical issues related to Christian doctrine. Williams questioned many of the Puritan laws in Massachusetts, especially the right of magistrates to punish Sabbath-breakers. Roger Williams and the Puritan magistrates disagreed about several important doctrinal issues:

The practice of forced church attendance. Williams could not agree with this Puritan practice. He believed that requiring church attendance, especially for those who were not sincerely religious, promoted hypocrisy. Echoing the words of the Apostle Paul, Williams pointed out, "An unbelieving soul is dead in sin." Therefore, to compel such a person to worship "was like shifting a dead man into several changes of apparel."[1]

Complete separation from the Church of England. Although the Pilgrims had separated from the Church of England, the Puritans were not complete separatists. Even their name reminds us that their hope was to purify the existing church. Oxford-trained Christian apologist, Os Guinness, points out that Williams "challenged the refusal of the [Puritan] church in America to separate officially from the Church of England."[2]

> *"God needeth not the help of a material sword of steel to assist the sword of the Spirit."*
>
> Roger Williams

Taking land from the Indians. Os Guinness also observes that Williams "criticized taking lands from the Indians, and he found himself in frequent conflict with John Winthrop and other leaders of Massachusetts."[3] Williams believed that the colonists should always purchase the land.

Requiring oaths. Because of the precarious nature of the relationship between the Massachusetts Bay Colony and Mother England, the Puritan leaders required all male citizens to take an oath, a pledge of loyalty, to them. This pledge of allegiance, called the freeman's oath, was made to the colony, not to King Charles. Williams believed this oath interfered with individual conscience. This conflict became the most significant point of contention between Williams and the Puritan fathers. Bancroft says: "The liberty of conscience, for which Williams contended, denied the right of a compulsory imposition of an oath: when, in March 1635, he was summoned before the court, he could not renounce his belief."[4]

Using the state to guard against heresy. Williams also disagreed with the Puritan practice of using civil magistrates to guard the spiritual purity of the church. Bancroft observes:

> [T]he controversy finally turned on the question of the rights and duty of magistrates to guard the minds of the people against corrupting influences, and to punish what would seem to them error and heresy. . . .

[C]onscience belongs to the individual, and is not the property of the body politic."[5]

Williams, who was the first to formulate the concept of "separation of church and state" in America, said: "[T]he civil magistrate may not intermeddle even to stop a church from apostasy and heresy."[6] President Thomas Jefferson echoed the idea of the "separation of church and state" in an 1802 letter to the Danbury Baptists of Connecticut, assuring them that the federal government would not interfere with their freedom of religion. It has only been in the last half century that America's courts have used this concept to keep all religious expression out of the public square under the guise of a prohibited First Amendment "establishment of religion."

Put Away Your Sword

Perhaps Roger Williams' most lasting and most significant legacy is that he promoted the (to us, obvious) notion that religious disputes should not be decided by the sword. Unfortunately, Christian history has been marred by those calling themselves Christians who think it is their duty to take up the sword for the sake of the Gospel. From the earliest days to the present, such conduct has always given Christianity a black eye, whether it be the Crusades, the Inquisition, or the Salem Witchcraft trials. Pure doctrine, in Roger Williams' view, could not be maintained by the force of the state.

> *"The colony [of Rhode Island] rested on the principle of intellectual liberty; philosophy itself could not have placed it on a broader basis."*
>
> Historian George Bancroft

Roger Williams was not proclaiming any new doctrine here. From the time Jesus told Peter to put away his sword, Christianity was intended to be spread and maintained by spiritual weapons. Martin Luther had said a century earlier: "I will preach, speak, write the truth, but will force it on no one, for faith must be accepted willingly, and without compulsion."[7] Luther had also condemned those who burned heretics at the stake, saying: "If fire is the right cure for heresy, then [those who light the wooden sticks for the fire] are the most learned doctors on earth; no need we study any more."[8]

Truth is the cornerstone of Christianity. When Jesus prayed for unity within the church, He prayed: "Sanctify them through thy truth, thy word is truth" (John 17:17). Christians are sanctified by the truth, and if we abide by Jesus' teaching the truth shall set us free (John 8:32).

Thus, the sword has no power to unify or protect the true church. Religious differences are not to be solved by the natural sword, but only by "the sword of God's spirit, the Word of God."[9] Roger Williams reminded his Christian brethren that returning to New Testament Christianity in its purist form meant serving the Prince of Peace and that those who live by the sword shall die by the sword.

These Biblical views promoted by Roger Williams protect people of all faiths who continue to come to America in our own time without fear of persecution. But if the Christian foundation for such protections is lost, what will become of us all?

Separation of Church and State

> "... Williams would permit persecution of no opinion, of no religion, leaving heresy unharmed by law, and orthodoxy unprotected by the terrors of penal statutes."
>
> Historian George Bancroft

In the 1643 charter for Rhode Island and in all its subsequent charters, Roger Williams established by law the idea that the state should not enforce religious opinion. He expressed these views in a letter he wrote in 1651 to Massachusetts Governor Endicott:

Sir, I must be humbly bold to say that 'tis impossible for any man or men to maintain their Christ by their sword and to worship a true Christ, to fight against all consciences opposite to theirs, and not to fight against God in some of them and to hunt after the precious life of the true Lord Jesus Christ.[10]

This philosophy leads naturally to a separation of the institution of the church from the institution of the state – a separation that was intended to benefit the church. Roger Williams very clearly based his doctrine of the separation of church and state on a Scriptural foundation. This doctrine of separation should not be confused in any way with the modern secular (mis)understanding of the separation of church and state. Roger Williams believed that the church and state were separate and distinct jurisdictions because the civil government may use the sword only to maintain the peace, not to impose doctrinal purity. Williams used the Bible's "Book of Judges" to demonstrate that even ancient Israel, despite all the advantages of being God's people, did a poor job of maintaining true religion by force.

The point modern separationists miss is that the religious liberty enjoyed in America is an outgrowth of Biblical doctrines. The Bible is the basis for true liberty, not its opponent, as some secularists today would have us believe. It is possible for the state to honor God, even to encourage religion, without imposing religious conformity or operating a state church in violation of the First Amendment prohibition against an "establishment of religion."

A Haven for the Free Conscience

Rhode Island was a sanctuary for religious dissidents. Roger Williams called his new settlement Providence to honor God for miraculously sparing his life during his winter flight to the colony and also to honor God's sovereignty over the affairs of man. At the very outset, he declared: "I desired . . . it might be for a shelter for persons distressed for conscience."[11] George Bancroft adds, "Within two years others fled to his asylum."[12] This was the beginning of the Rhode Island colony, where "God alone was respected as the Ruler of conscience."[13]

Roger Williams' greatest contribution to our modern doctrines of religious liberty was his insistence upon the freedom of conscience. George Bancroft points out:

> Roger Williams asserted the great doctrine of intellectual liberty, and made it the corner-stone of a political constitution. It became his glory to found a state upon that principle, and to stamp himself upon its rising institutions, in characters so deep that the impress has remained to the present day.[14]

Writing about the Biblical ideal of not using the force of the state to coerce religious uniformity, Williams asserted:

> The God of Peace, the God of Truth will shortly seal this truth, and confirm this witness, and make it evident to the whole world, that the doctrine of persecution for cause of conscience, is most evidently and lamentably contrary to the doctrine of Christ Jesus the Prince of Peace.[15]

Bancroft explains: "Williams was willing to leave Truth alone, in her own panoply of light, believing that, if in the ancient feud between Truth and Error the employment of force could be entirely abrogated, Truth would have much the best of the bargain."[16] In other words, let truth be proclaimed without force and truth will always win.

William Penn

Among the religious refugees who came to these shores in the 17th century were followers of George Fox, better known as Quakers. They were first labeled as such because they "tremble[d] at the word of God."[17] The most important Quaker in America was William Penn, whose name has been forever enshrined in the annals of our history. The state generally associated with him – Pennsylvania, meaning "Penn's woods" or "Penn's forest" – was actually named for his father.

Personal History

William Penn (1644-1718), born in London, was the son of a British naval officer – Sir William Penn. At the age of eleven, the young William had a strong Christian experience that would affect the rest of his life and would lead directly to his strong belief that every person has the God-given right to determine how he will worship and with whom he will fellowship.

> "... it still matters what Penn did two hundred years ago or what Franklin did a hundred years ago; I never could feel in New York that it mattered what anybody did an hour ago."
>
> G. K. Chesterton,
> *What I Saw in America*

Penn received an excellent education, but he was expelled from Christ Church at Oxford because of his dissenting Christian views, which were not in conformity with the prevailing views of the Church of England. His father then sent him to France to study abroad and, hopefully, shake his nonconformist religious convictions. But Penn studied among the Huguenots, who were themselves being persecuted because they were French Calvinists. His relationship with the Huguenots only confirmed young William's dissenting religious views. He returned to England to study law, but when the Plague broke out in 1665, his studies were cut short.

Penn, now a young man, learned to manage lands and people by managing his father's estate in Ireland. He also became friends with the founder of the Quakers, George Fox, and became an apologist for the new Quaker faith. Penn often spent time in prison because of his dissenting religious views. He wrote extensively during these times of imprisonment.

Penn's great love for liberty and his striving after religious freedom were already the driving focus of his life when he began to correspond with Roger Williams of Rhode Island. Even though Rev. Williams strongly disagreed with

Penn's theology, he thoroughly supported Penn's right to follow his own conscience. Penn traveled extensively all over England and on the European continent visiting Quakers. He even made the acquaintance of John Locke, the accomplished European philosopher.

It became clear to Penn that the Quakers, also called Friends, were not only mistreated in England, but also in some colonies of the New World. He found this mistreatment to be especially troubling in Massachusetts, where four Quakers had been put to death. While the death penalty was later dropped against Quakers in New England, the stories from Boston were quite disturbing, and Penn protested this treatment to the colonial authorities.

The New Jersey Concessions

From 1674-1680, William Penn was asked to serve as an arbiter a land conflict regarding West New Jersey in the New World. The dispute was between two English Quakers, Ed Billing and John Fenwick. Penn's legal training and experience managing land in Ireland helped him resolve the matter. In 1675, Fenwick decided to take a group of Quakers to the New World to settle this piece of land.

> *To bring "savage Natives by gentle and just manners to the love of civil society and Christian religion."*
>
> One of the goals of Pennsylvania, as conceived by its founder

William Penn was the main author of the founding governmental document for this land, called *The Concessions*, which was not only governmental in nature but was also concerned with social, philosophical, scientific, and political matters. By 1680, *The Concessions* had 150 signers, and in the Quaker spirit, this group effort provided for far-reaching liberties never before seen in Anglo-Saxon law. Here is an excerpt of what they wrote:

> We have made concessions by ourselves . . . [and] we lay a foundation for after ages to understand their liberty as men and Christians, that they may not be brought in bondage, but by their own consent; *for we put the power in the people,* that is to say, they to meet and choose one honest man for each proprietary, who hath subscribed to *The Concessions;* all these men to meet as an assembly there, to make and repeal laws, to choose a governor, or commissioner, and twelve assistants to execute the laws during their pleasure; so every man is capable to choose or be chosen. No man to be arrested, condemned, imprisoned, or molested in his estate or liberty, but by twelve men

of the neighborhood. No man to lie in prison for debt, but that his estate satisfy as far as it will go, and be set at liberty to work. No person to be called in question or molested for his conscience, or for worshiping according to his conscience.[18]

These *Concessions* demonstrate that another sect of Christianity, operating in the New World out of the same Biblical principles as others before it, was giving birth to liberty and to the political concept of the consent of the governed. This was a radical notion in its day. In many parts of the world (generally in non-Christianized nations) it is still a radical notion in our own day, more than three hundred years later.

> "There is one great God and Power that hath made the world and all things therein, to whom you and I and all people owe their being and well-being, and to whom you and I must one day given an account, for all that we doe in the world."
>
> William Penn,
> in a letter to Indians

To these *Concessions* was added this proposition: "That no man nor number of men upon earth hath power or authority to rule over men's consciences in religious matters."[19] Under these *Concessions*, the Indians were also encouraged to bring their problems to the commissioners and to have a fair trial before a court of six Indians and six settlers. Catherine Owens Peare, Penn's biographer, reflected upon the success of the colony and its government based upon Biblical principles:

The social experiment in a rankless community, where the right of self-determination of every individual was sacred, where God was the final source of authority, succeeded and prospered, and it did so on the simple formula: love-industry-integrity.[20]

Pennsylvania is Born

When Charles II reluctantly allowed limited parliamentary elections in England in 1679, William Penn's neighbor and friend, Algernon Sydney, ran for a seat, arguing that the power of government must never be in the hands of just one person. Sydney was opposed to the divine right of kings. Penn worked as his friend's campaign manager, but Sydney lost the election under unfair circumstances.[21] Sydney's governmental ideals were set forth in his *Discourses Concerning Government* (1698), a treatise that greatly influenced political thought in 18th century America. Eventually, Sydney was falsely accused of insurrection and was executed in England.

The political situation in England was becoming intolerable, especially for religious and political dissenters. By 1680, Penn saw no future for the Friends in England. In light of the success of the New Jersey experiment, he decided that a colony in America would be the only solution.

While King Charles disapproved of Penn's dissenting religious views, the monarchy owed a debt to Penn's father. Therefore, in May 1680, the king presented to William Penn the title to the land we now know as Pennsylvania as a repayment of that debt. King Charles also saw this gift as a way of getting rid of a troublesome political opponent. The documents giving Pennsylvania to William Penn were finalized in 1681. While Penn thought it vain, the name *Pennsylvania* was chosen for this land grant by King Charles II to honor Penn's father, Sir William, who had been a friend of the Crown.

> *"Liberty without obedience is confusion, and obedience without liberty is slavery."*
>
> William Penn

Penn now sought visionary men to go to Pennsylvania – those who were brave and adventurous with a variety of talents and skills. One of those selected was Robert Turner, a Dublin merchant and long-time Quaker and friend. In a letter to Turner, Penn wrote of his vision for the new colony (his "country"):

[A]fter many waitings, watchings, solicitings, and disputes in council, my country was confirmed to me under the great seal of England. God will bless it and make it the seed of a nation. I shall have a tender care of the government, that it be well laid at first.[22]

Preparations for the New Colony

Penn's idealistic plans for the new government proposed liberties that were far ahead of his time, including the division of powers and the right to self-government. The cry for religious freedom at that time must be understood in the context of the oppressive Church of England. Settlers to the New World were not seeking freedom from Christianity, but freedom from the tyranny of a coercive state church. Freedom under God, with self-government and the right of every man to think and believe and worship as he saw fit – that was the great vision that led William Penn to undertake the task of building a new colony.

Penn, who initially remained in England, sent a general letter to the people who were settling the new colony, outlining his vision:

You shall be governed by laws of your own [making], and live a free, and if you will, [as] a sober and industrious People. I shall not usurp the right of any, or oppress his person.[23]

Just as he had done in the New Jersey *Concessions*, Penn was placing governmental power in the hands of the people. With the help of his friends, Penn drafted the first documents for the government of Pennsylvania before he had ever seen the land. In the twenty articles known as Penn's *Frame of Government*, the first ten concerned the land; the next five dealt with the just treatment of the Indians, and the last five were concerned with the laws.

Before Penn ever departed from England to the New World himself, refugees began to pour into his newly framed colony. The earliest settlers came from England, Ireland, and Wales. Later, others arrived from France, Germany, and Holland. Land could be bought or rented, but it had to be planted within three years.

Penn's next project involved a unique concept of a city with well-laid plans. In true renaissance spirit, he employed the ancient Greek idea of a planned city with straight streets intersecting at right angles. This plan became the city of Philadelphia, the city of brotherly love. Such city planning had been done by several kings in Europe in the 1600s. Penn assigned to Thomas Holm the responsibility of selecting a site and laying out the streets of Philadelphia.

> *"This great God hath written His law in our hearts by which we are taught and commanded to love and help and doe good to one another and not to doe harm and mischief one unto another."*
>
> William Penn

Penn's Frame of Government

The greatness of William Penn shines in his framing of the government of Pennsylvania. He sought the counsel of other learned men and he signed away all personal power. Both of these things are very difficult for any ambitious person to do. Furthermore, Penn set up the government in such a way that neither he, nor his descendants, could ever abuse political power. To this day, the Historical Society of Pennsylvania possesses nineteen of the early manuscripts that helped to provide for the framing of the government of Pennsylvania.

These documents deal primarily with liberty of conscience and with political arrangements. They were drafted by many hands, but notes in William Penn's own handwriting show how carefully he studied the advice of his friends and colleagues. Penn biographer, Catherine Owens Peare, writes:

> *The Frame of Government*, that went through so many conferences and
> revisions before its approval by the First Adventurers and William Penn
> consisted of two parts: a document with a Preface and twenty-four sections
> which Penn specifically called *The Frame* signed by Penn April 20,1682, and
> a body of forty laws signed by Penn on May 5, 1682. Penn blanketed them
> under the one long title, *The Frame of Government of the Province of
> Pennsylvania, in America, Together with Certain Laws Agreed Upon in England,
> by the Governor and Divers Freemen of the Aforesaid Province, to be Further
> Explained, and Continued There by the First Provincial Council That Shall be
> Held, if They See Meet.*[24]

Religion and government are so intertwined in this document that it is
impossible to separate them. To hold public office, one had to be a Christian, but
there were no restrictions on denominational affiliation. Furthermore, like Roger
Williams' colony in Rhode Island, no one could be "molested or prejudiced for
their religious persuasion, or practice, in matters of faith and worship, nor shall
they be compelled, at any time, to frequent or maintain any religious worship,
place or ministry whatsoever."[25]

While freedom of religion was very important – especially the freedom to
worship as conscience would dictate – morality was also important. Peare
comments:

> Penn held morality of supreme importance to the success of a state and several
> of the laws forbade corruption, fraud, bribery, extortion, slander, and a long list
> of offenses against God including swearing, lying, drunkenness, incest, sodomy,
> whoredom, duels, felony, bull- and bear-baiting, cockfights and any things
> "which excite the people to rudeness, cruelty, looseness and irreligion."[26]

It is very clear that what Penn envisioned for his colony was not freedom
from religion, but freedom *of* religion – not a separation of government from all
religion, but a government that respected the religious consciences of all its
citizens. He envisioned a place where every man was free, not to live an ungodly
life, but to practice his religion in peace, to have the right to rule his own estate,
and to participate in making laws and enforcing them. Individual freedom could
only work if the people were self-governed and industrious. That statement is as
true today as it was in 1680.

Penn pictured government as a clock, a mechanism that men wound up and set in motion. Evil men could ruin a good government, and good men could make even a bad government work. Any government is only as good as its people.

Settling in Pennsylvania

Finally, having laid so many careful plans in advance, William Penn was ready to go to Pennsylvania. But before leaving England, Penn was offered a temptation to deny his principles and make some illicit money, money he sorely needed. Traders offered him 6,000 pounds plus annual pay for "a monopoly of the Indian traffic between the Delaware and the Susquehannah."[27]

But Penn was a dedicated Christian, a man of principles, who could not be bought. His *Frame of Government* made such practices illegal, and he refused to violate the rights of the Indians. He turned the offer down, declaring:

> I will not abuse the love of God . . . nor act unworthy of his Providence, by defiling what came to me clean. No; let the Lord guide me by his wisdom to honor his name and serve his truth and people, that an example and a standard may be set up to the nations. [28]

Nearly a hundred Quakers sailed with Penn in 1682 to join the earlier settlers in the new province of Pennsylvania. Within the first year after they arrived, Penn made a peace treaty with the Indians. He bought land from them, included them in juries, and assured them of fair trials. Under the great treaty of Shackamaxon, the Indians and the settlers lived together in peace for about seventy years.

Not since the time of the Pilgrims and Roger Williams had any colonial leader taken justice for the Indians so seriously, but Penn believed it was the Christian thing to do.

Penn's Legacy

Pennsylvania was instrumental in securing religious liberty in America. The Pennsylvania State House, now called Independence Hall in Philadelphia, is the place where both the Declaration of Independence and the United States Constitution were drafted and signed.

Paul Johnson said that at the time of America's founding, Philadelphia was "the cultural capital of America."[29] He also points out: "It can be argued, indeed, that Quaker Pennsylvania was the key state in American history. It was the last great flowering of Puritan political innovation, around its great city of brotherly love."[30] What William Penn established remains to this day.

William Penn would likely remind us today, just as he reminded the early settlers of Pennsylvania: "I beseech God to direct you in the way of righteousness, and therein prosper you and your children after you."[31] This is a warning we should heed in our own time in order that we, like William Penn and his friend Roger Williams, might have liberty under God to do what is right.

Every Bible-believing Christian should honor the memories of Roger Williams and William Penn. They left a long-lasting legacy of religious and civil liberties and of freedom of conscience. Neither man's life was easy, but both left the world a much better place than they found it. They exemplify the proposition that America is, in large part, the product of religious nonconformists.

Other Early Nonconformists

In centuries past, it took conviction, strong faith, and courage to be a nonconformist and a religious dissenter. Beyond the Pilgrims, Puritans, and Quakers, there were other religious dissidents fleeing persecution in the Old World. In the first part of the 18th century, hundreds of thousands of Scotch-Irish Presbyterians fled from England and English-held territories, as had Roman Catholics, although in much smaller numbers beginning in the 1600s. There were the Huguenots, fleeing persecution in France. There were Anabaptists, fleeing persecution in Germany. Christians of all backgrounds found their way to these shores, fleeing religious persecution from oppressive state churches all over Europe.

These nonconformists were not fleeing from religion or from the right to live as Christians in an organized society, as some secularists today would have us think. Instead, they were fleeing from abuse and religious persecution by state-established churches, and they were also seeking the right to establish their own communities under the laws of God, as they understood them.

Maryland's Tolerance Act

While Catholics persecuted Protestants in France and Protestants persecuted Catholics in England, persecuted Christians of all kinds found refuge in America. In 1649, the Catholic colony of Maryland (named after the wife of Charles I, not after the Mother of Jesus as could be surmised) introduced a religious toleration act.

The Maryland Toleration Act, in the words of Paul Johnson, allowed for "the free practice of religion but made it an offense to use hostile language about the religion of others, 'such as Heretick, Schismatic, Idolator, Puritan, Independent, Presbyterian, Popish Priest, Jesuite, Jesuited Papist, Roundhead, Separatist and the like.'"[32] A fine was imposed on anyone who used a derogatory religious label against another citizen.

Before there was freedom for all religions in America, there was religious freedom for Christians of all denominations. Christianity was the religion that gave birth to religious liberty for everyone. Even today, as Christian America welcomes refugees of all religions or of no religion, in those parts of the world where the Christian Gospel has not had a sizable influence, there is little religious liberty or any other type of civil liberties. The only exceptions to this rule are nations like Japan, where the government has been patterned after Western democracies founded on the Gospel.

> "*The whole inspiration of our civilization springs from the teachings of Christ and the lessons of the prophets. To read the Bible for these fundamentals is a necessity of American life.*"
>
> Herbert Hoover,
> 31st President

The Influence of John Calvin

John Calvin greatly influenced the founding of America. Some historians have even gone so far as to call him "the founder of America."[33] In fact, although Calvin never lived in America, his theological influence on the founding of America was profound. It was Calvin's stress on "covenant theology" that provided much of the framework for the covenants, compacts, constitutions, and bodies of liberty, which ultimately culminated in the U.S. Constitution.

American Calvinists

A key Calvinist doctrine that influenced early Americans was the sovereignty of God over all spheres of life. Calvinists emphasized the belief that Jesus should not just be Lord of their personal spiritual lives, but that He should also be Lord over every sphere of life – including politics and government. Their belief that the Lord superintends every area of life caused these American Calvinists to form governments in the New World that respected religious liberty, while at the same time including Biblical principles in all aspects of personal, social, and political life.

Abraham Kuyper, a great Dutch theologian and staunch Calvinist who served as prime minister of the Netherlands, summarized Calvinism by focusing on Jesus Christ as the Son of God:

The Son is not to be excluded from anything. You cannot point to any natural realm or star or comet or even descend into the depth of the earth, but it is related to Christ, not in some unimportant tangential way, but directly. There is no force in nature, no laws that control those forces that do not have their origin in that eternal Word. For this reason, it is totally false to restrict Christ to spiritual affairs and to assert that there is no point of contact between him and the natural sciences.[34]

Dr. Loraine Boettner, a Christian scholar who has sometimes been quoted by the U.S. Supreme Court, observed: "[T]wo-thirds of the population [at the time of the Revolution] had been trained in the school of Calvin."[35] Dr. Boettner wrote an overview of the Christian commitment of the colonists in the 1776 era:

Never in the world's history had a nation been founded by such people as these. Furthermore these people came to America not primarily for commercial gain or advantage, but because of deep religious convictions. It seems that the religious persecutions in various European countries had been providentially used to select out the most progressive and enlightened people for the colonization of America.[36]

> *"It would be hard to overrate the debt which mankind owes to Calvin. The spiritual father of Coligny, of William the Silent, and of Cromwell, must occupy a foremost rank among the champions of modern democracy."*
>
> Historian John Fiske,
> *Beginnings of New England*

Historian George Bancroft labeled the American War for Independence as a Presbyterian phenomenon:

The Revolution of 1776, so far as it was affected by religion was a Presbyterian measure. It was the natural out growth of the principles which the Presbyterianism of the Old World planted in her sons, the English Puritans, the Scotch Covenanters, the French Huguenots, the Dutch Calvinists, and the Presbyterians of Ulster.[37]

Many in England placed the blame for the revolution directly upon the Presbyterian passion for liberty. Lorraine Boettner explains:

So intense, universal, and aggressive were the Presbyterians in their zeal for liberty that the war was spoken of in England as "The Presbyterian Rebellion."

An ardent colonial supporter of King George III wrote home: "I fix all the blame for these extraordinary proceedings upon the Presbyterians. They have been the chief and principal instruments in all these flaming measures. They always do and ever will act against government from that restless and turbulent anti-monarchial spirit which has always distinguished them everywhere."[38]

During the Revolutionary War, the British Prime Minister, Horace Walpole, remarked to Parliament, "Cousin America has run off with a Presbyterian parson."[39] That Presbyterian "parson" was Rev. John Witherspoon, the president of Princeton, a signer of the Declaration of Independence as a delegate from New Jersey.

> *"The Presbyterians, with their Calvinist view of limited government and the duty to resist tyranny, were among the nation's strongest supporters of independence."*
>
> John Eidsmoe

Conclusion

Most of the Presbyterians who came to America in the 1700s were already familiar with representative self-government in their churches. The Presbyterian framework for church government contributed directly to the framework for America's political system. As Dr. E. W. Smith said: "When the fathers of our Republic sat down to frame a system of representative and popular government ... their task was not so difficult as some have imagined. They had a model to work by."[40] Calvin gave to the world: "a republican spirit in religion, with the kindred principles of republican liberty."[41]

Our second President John Adams was convinced that the strong influence of Christianity had shaped American republicanism. He wrote:

> The general Principles, on which the Fathers Achieved Independence, were the only Principles in which that beautiful Assembly of young Gentlemen could Unite, and those Principles only could be intended by them in their Address, or by me in my Answer. And what were these general Principles? I answer, the general Principles of Christianity, in which all those Sects were United: and the general Principles of English and American liberty, in which all those young Men United, and which had United all Parties in America.[42]

The fourth thing every Christian should know about the founding of

America is that the Pilgrims, Puritans, Quakers, and other religious dissidents who founded settlements in the New World were seeking asylum from religious persecution. They were also seeking the opportunity to live in freedom under the laws of God in the American wilderness. America began as a loosely knit group of Christian dissidents.

Chapter 5
The Beginning of Wisdom

"The fear of the Lord is the beginning of knowledge . . . "
~ Proverbs 1:7a

The education of the settlers and founders of America was uniquely Christian and Bible-based.

illions of Americans alive today learned to read using such profound statements as "See Jane, run. Run, Jane, run." or "See Spot. See Spot play. Play, Spot, play." This is quite a contrast to the first reading material our founders used. The fifth thing every Christian should know about the founding of America is that the education of the settlers and founders of America was uniquely Christian and Bible-based.

The little colonial student in early America marched off to his one-room schoolhouse and opened his new reading primer, but instead of reading about Jane and Spot, our little colonial friend was taught to read using magnificent truths based on the Word of God. Here is one example:

An Alphabet of Lessons for Youth.

A Wise son maketh a glad father, but a foolish son is the heaviness of his mother.

Better is a little with the fear of the Lord, than great treasure & trouble therewith.

Come unto Christ all ye that labor and are heavy laden and he will give you rest.[1]

When American children during the colonial era learned their ABC's, they also learned sound Bible doctrine. During its first two hundred years, education in America was thoroughly Christian. The Bible was the chief textbook, and the children learned it well. By the turn of the 19th century, John Adams could state that finding an illiterate man in New England was as rare as a comet.[2] Today, by contrast, the skies over America seem to be filled with comets.

Virtually every Founding Father received a Christian education based on the Bible. In fact, from the very beginning of Christian settlements in this land, a Christian education was a very important part of colonial life for the average child, both in his formative years and later in college if he attended. Our Founding Fathers were educated from a Christian worldview. David Barton, author and speaker on America's Christian heritage, points out that more than 40 percent of the signers of the Declaration of Independence (24 of 56) had seminary degrees.[3]

The settlers and founders of this country had a Christian worldview derived from a vigorous Christian education. Tragically, in contrast, some of what is called "Christian education" today is essentially a secular worldview with a thin veneer of spirituality to make it appear Christian. In today's public schools, even the thin veneer is gone.

> *"The New England Primer, introduced in Boston in 1690 by Benjamin Harris, was the first textbook printed in America."*
>
> David Barton

The Christian education our founders received was thoroughly Biblical at its core. Even the least religious of the Founding Fathers, such as Benjamin Franklin and Thomas Jefferson, were regular readers of the Bible. The political writings of the founders are heavily sprinkled with Scriptural quotations and allusions. The early colonists were Biblically literate, and our Founding Fathers knew they were speaking to a Biblically literate audience.

The Old Deluder Act

The Puritans and other God-fearing colonists were firm believers in education. They instituted schools virtually from the very beginning of their settlements. Historian George Bancroft writes:

> It was ever the custom, and, in 1642, it became the law, in Puritan New England, that "none of the brethren shall suffer so much barbarism in their families as not to teach their children and apprentices so much learning as may

enable them perfectly to read the English tongue."[4]

In 1647, in each Puritan colony, it was thus ordered:

To the end that learning may not be buried in the graves of our forefathers . . .
every township, after the Lord hath increased them to the number of fifty
householders, shall appoint one to teach all children to read and write; and
where any town shall increase to the number of one hundred families, they
shall set up a grammar school, the masters thereof being able to instruct youth
so far as they may be fitted for the university.[5]

> *"It being one chief project
> of that old deluder,
> Satan, to keep men from
> the knowledge of the
> Scriptures, as in former
> times by keeping them in
> an unknown tongue . . .
> It is therefore ordered
> that every township in
> this jurisdiction, after
> the Lord hath increased
> them to fifty households
> shall forthwith appoint
> one within their town to
> teach all such children..."*
>
> The Old Deluder Act, 1647

This new law was called the Old Deluder Act because it was intended to defeat Satan, the Old Deluder, who had used illiteracy in the Old World to keep people from reading the Word of God. The main purpose of schools in Puritan New England was to teach children to read the Bible.

Education for the Primary Grades

The *New England Primer*, the book used to teach colonial children to read, included the Lord's Prayer, the Apostle's Creed, and the text of many hymns and prayers by Isaac Watts. John Adams, Samuel Adams, John Hancock, Elbridge Gerry (from whom we get the word gerrymandering), and hundreds of thousands of other early colonists learned their ABC's from this powerful, tiny book. Here is one lesson from the *New England Primer* entitled "A Lesson for Children:"

Pray to God.
Love God.
Fear God.
Serve God.
Take not God's
  Name in Vain.
Do not Swear.
Do not Steal.
Cheat not in your play.

Call no ill names.
Use no ill words.
Tell no lies.
Hate Lies.
Speak the Truth.
Spend your Time well.
Love your School.
Mind your Book.
Strive to learn.

Play not with bad boys.   Be not a Dunce.[6]

How refreshing such wonderful lessons would be in our public schools today. These are timeless truths that all the early settlers and founders of this country were taught as children.

When colonial children learned the alphabet, they also learned key messages from the Bible. There was more Biblical truth imparted in the *New England Primer* for early American school children than is probably preached in the average American church pulpit today. Here is another example of how these children learned the alphabet:

A
In ADAM'S Fall
We sinned all.
B
Heaven to find;
The Bible Mind.
C
Christ crucify'd
For sinners dy'd.[7]

> *"I am much afraid that schools will prove to be the great gates of hell unless they diligently labor in explaining the Holy Scriptures, engraving them in the hearts of youth."*
>
> Martin Luther

The lesson book then went on to teach the children a Christian catechism. Keep in mind that the *New England Primer* was not a textbook for the elite. It was used in towns and even in backwoods regions by frontiersmen. It was the primary textbook for American school children for more than a century and was used widely throughout New England and beyond.

The Northwest Ordinance
Some modern secularists attempt to argue that even though the early settlers were Christian (the Puritans, Pilgrims, Huguenots, etc.), by the time of the Revolutionary War, the Founding Fathers intended to establish a secular state. The problem with this misreading of history is that it does not match the facts. There is a preponderance of evidence to the contrary, including in the realm of education.

The first United States Congress meeting under the new Constitution in 1789 passed a law directing that each additional state and territory to be added to the new nation should be committed to building schools. This law was a re-enactment of a law that had been previously passed on July 13, 1787, while the nation was still being governed by the Articles of Confederation. The American experiment could only work if the people were taught to read and write. So, on August 4, 1789, the same Congress that enacted the Bill of Rights with its First Amendment, also re-enacted the Northwest Ordinance.[8] The Northwest at that time referred to the expanding territory north and west of the Appalachians. The Northwest Ordinance is one of America's founding documents, and it was applied to all new territories and states of the United States.

One provision included in the Northwest Ordinance is most instructive, considering that it was enacted by the very same Congress that gave us the First Amendment Establishment Clause, which is now being interpreted by courts to require a complete separation of church and state (including keeping religion out of public education). The provision states:

> *"A well-instructed people alone can be permanently a free people."*
>
> James Madison,
> Second Annual Message to
> Congress, Dec. 5, 1810

Religion, morality, and knowledge being necessary to good government and the happiness of mankind, schools and the means of education shall forever be encouraged.[9]

Many states that later joined the union used this same language in their new state constitutions. For example, the Mississippi state constitution (1817) says:

Article IX, Section 16 Religion, morality, and knowledge, being necessary to good government, the preservation of liberty and the happiness of mankind, schools and the means of education shall be forever encouraged in this state.[10]

The Northwest Ordinance demonstrates that the founders of America intended that education, religion, and morality should work hand-in-hand in order to guarantee good government and preserve liberty.

America's First College

Most people know that Harvard was America's first college. Many do not know that the college was named for the *Reverend* John Harvard or that, for its first few hundred years of existence, it was a distinctly Christian college.

The school was founded in 1636, barely six years after the Puritans first began to colonize Massachusetts. The Puritans obviously made education a very high priority. Historian, Puritan, and noted author, Cotton Mather, who attended Harvard in his early teen years, points out that the motive for establishing the school was to train ministers of the Gospel:

> [T]he Christians in the most early times of New-England were to form a colledge, wherein a succession of a learned and able ministry might be educated. And, indeed, they foresaw that without such a provision for a *sufficient ministry*, the churches of New-England must have been less than a *business of one age*, and soon have come to nothing: the other *hemisphere* of the world would never have sent us over men enough to have answered our necessities; but without a nursery for such men among ourselves "darkness must have covered the land, and gross darkness the people."[11]

This vision for Harvard was born on September 8, 1630 – within the first year of the Puritan's arrival. Some Puritan leaders held a general council on that date in Boston and conceived the idea for a university, advancing a "small sum" to that end of four hundred pounds. Mather notes this inconspicuous beginning: "[I]t was then a day of small things."[12]

> *"Promote . . . as an object of primary importance institutions for the general diffusion of knowledge."*
>
> George Washington, "Farewell Address"

The new town where the college was to be built was originally named *Kiriath Sepher*, the City of Books. But the name was changed to Cambridge, observes Paul Johnson, in honor of Cambridge, in England, where Rev. Harvard had gone to school.[13]

Not much is known about Rev. John Harvard (1607-1638) except that he was a young minister who died of consumption (tuberculosis) soon after he arrived from England – two years after the school had been established in 1636. Cotton Mather says he was "a reverend and excellent minister of the gospel." [14] His will granted seven hundred, seventy-nine pounds, seventeen shillings, and two pence for the "pious work" to be built in Cambridge.[15] He also donated 400 books for the library.

To honor his memory, the General Court of Massachusetts named the school after Rev. Harvard. His generous donation helped construct some of the buildings for the new school. The library was founded in 1638 with his donated books and is now the oldest library in the United States.

Ironically, the first teacher at Harvard, Nathaniel Eaton, was not a man of good character. He was deceptive, cruel, and a lover of money. One day, he hammered away at a student with a cudgel (a club or mallet), was hauled into court, and was fined a hundred marks. He was removed from his post and excommunicated from the church. He then went to Virginia and on back to England, where he became "a bitter persecutor of the Christians that kept faithful to the way of worship."[16]

Harvard Laws of 1643

We can learn a lot about Harvard by looking at some of its earliest rules, such as the Laws and Statutes for Students of Harvard College, 1643, which begins by stating: "Let every student be plainly instructed and earnestly pressed to consider well the main end of his life and studies is *to know God and Jesus Christ which is eternal life* (John 17:3)."[17] While it may seem shocking today, Harvard's purpose in 1643 was to lead students to know God the Father and to know His Son, Jesus Christ.

The rules go on to stipulate that students were required to read and study the Bible at least twice a day. They were to show the utmost respect to God's ordinances, to memorize the Scriptures and be able to recite these publicly if called upon by their teachers. God's Holy Name was to be used reverently. No profanity was allowed. Students were to attend their classes and chapel services "without any disturbance by word or gesture."[18] Furthermore, the rules continue: "None shall under any pretense whatsoever frequent the company and society of such men as lead an unfit and dissolute life."[19]

> *"And although this country did chiefly consist of such as, by the difficulties of subduing a wretched wilderness, were brought into such a condition of poverty . . . yet [they] were willing to let the richer colonies, which retained the ways of the Church of England, see 'how much true religion was a friend unto good literature.'"*
>
> Cotton Mather

The students were expected to know Latin, the language of most theological writings at that time. They were also expected to know Hebrew and Greek in order to translate the Scriptures from their original languages.

Imagine if these rules were implemented at Harvard today. There would almost assuredly be a riot on the campus.

Harvard was a thoroughly Christian institution during its first two centuries – strongly evangelical and Bible-based, but the school began to change during the early 19th century under the influence of Unitarianism. Although Harvard was explicitly Christian for more than two hundred years, it has been secular for only about the past hundred and fifty years. The change to secularism was a slow transition. A little compromise here. A minor change there. It did not happen overnight.

Many graduates of Harvard accomplished great things for God's glory. The school has had a great impact in America and in the world for Christ. It still continues to have a great impact today, but not generally for the glory of God as it once did.

Early Presidents of Harvard

William J. Federer, who compiled *America's God and Country*, a reference book for Christian patriots, points out that prior to America's War for Independence, ten of the twelve presidents of Harvard were ministers of the Gospel of Jesus Christ.[20]

> *"Avoid pride, sloth, and antichrist."*
>
> Admonition to an early Harvard graduation by Monsieur Guitton

After a partially bumpy start (as seen in the case of Mr. Eaton, its first teacher), the first great president of Harvard was Charles Chancey, who led the school for almost 20 years, from 1654-1671. Rev. Increase Mather, Cotton's father, spoke at his funeral – in Latin, which is a good indication of how well-educated the Puritans generally were.[21]

Later, Rev. Increase Mather became president of the school. He would often represent the Massachusetts colony back home in Mother England. One of the things that particularly troubled him on these many trips abroad in the late 17th century was seeing liberalism begin to creep into the colleges of Europe. He condemned "those Protestant universities, abroad in the world, which have not preserved the glorious *doctrines of grace* in such purity."[22]

One can only imagine what Increase Mather would think of Harvard today – with its anti-Christian curriculum, and its divinity school embracing every New Age idea or Eastern religion under the sun, while denigrating Western (that is, Judeo-Christian) religion.[23]

Harvard Graduates

It is clear that Harvard has had a great impact on the history of the United States, mostly for good. Quite a few of our presidents were trained at Harvard, including John Adams, John Quincy Adams, Theodore Roosevelt, Franklin D. Roosevelt, John F. Kennedy, Rutherford B. Hayes, and George W. Bush, who went to Harvard Graduate School. Even in its first century, Cotton Mather could point to the enormous influence Harvard graduates were having for God:

> In the perusal of this catalogue [listing Harvard alumni], it will be found that, besides a supply of ministers for our churches from this happy seminary, we have hence had a supply of magistrates, as well as physicians, and other gentlemen, to serve the commonwealth with their capacities.[24]

This provision of so many professionals beyond the clergy who studied in a thoroughly Christian school is very consistent with the Puritan worldview. Dedicated Christians were not merely intended to serve God as ministers. They were also intended to serve Him in politics, in law, in medicine, and in other "secular" professions. The Puritans believed that whatever field God called a Christian to pursue, he should pursue it vigorously for the glory of God.

Written in Stone

Today at Harvard, one can still find the following words etched in stone (written in old English):

> After God had carried us safe to New England, and we had built our houses, provided necessaries for our livelihood, reared convenient places for God's worship, and settled the civil government, one of the next things we longed for and looked after was to advance learning and perpetuate it to posterity; dreading to leave an illiterate ministry to the churches, when our present ministers shall lie in the dust.[25]

Secularists did not establish Harvard, and their take-over of the institution was a long time in coming. But since the 1800s, Harvard, the school with such an auspicious and Christian beginning, has slowly begun to wreak spiritual havoc instead of blessing. Those who have brought down this great and Godly institution will have much to account for before the Lord. Its downward path should serve as a warning for today's Christian colleges and universities.

Other Christian Colleges

There were other American schools of higher education founded for the glory of God. In fact, all of what are now called the Ivy League schools were Christian in origin, a fact that is not easily recognized today unless one finds the obscure etched stone or notices the cathedral-like buildings that dot these campuses. Dr. D. James Kennedy and Jerry Newcombe point out: "Almost every one of the first 123 colleges and universities in the United States has Christian origins."[26]

William and Mary

The second university or college in the colonies was William and Mary, founded in 1693 and named for the popular British monarchs who, in 1688, during the Glorious Revolution in England, had established the supremacy of Parliamentary rule over the monarchy. In 1779, William and Mary became the first college in the United States to "offer professional training in [the] law."[27]

William and Mary trained several American presidents, including Thomas Jefferson and John Tyler. The school was also the first to create Phi Beta Kappa to recognize top scholars and the honor system, which made students responsible for honest conduct in class.

William and Mary was founded as a Anglican college in which Jesus Christ was pre-eminent. The Statutes of the College of William and Mary from 1727 were clear in their spiritual intent:

> There are three things which the Founders of this College proposed to themselves, to which all its Statutes should be directed.
>
> The first is that the youth of Virginia should be well educated to learning and good morals.
>
> The second is that the churches of America, especially Virginia, should be supplied with good ministers after the doctrine and government of the Church of England, and that the college should be a constant seminary for this purpose.
>
> The Third is that the Indians of America should be instructed in the Christian religion, and that some of the Indian youth that are well behaved and well inclined, being first well prepared in the Divinity School, may be sent out to preach the gospel to their countrymen in their own tongue, after they have duly been put in orders of deacons and priests.[28]

Thomas Jefferson attended William and Mary and received a thoroughly Christian college education there.

Yale

Soon after the Puritans established their first settlement at Hartford, Connecticut, they established a second settlement in New Haven. Ten esteemed clergymen from the colony of New Haven assembled in 1700 at the nearby town of Branford. Each minister placed a few volumes on the table, donating them to found a new university, each one saying: "I give these books for the founding of a college in this colony."[29]

The next year, in 1701, the General Assembly of Connecticut – a thoroughly Christian and Puritan body – formed a charter for the school. For the first five years, classes met near the home of a minister, Rector Abraham Pierson of Killingsworth (now called Clinton).

Elihu Yale (1649-1721), a wealthy Puritan who made his fortune through the East India Tea Company, regularly made generous donations to "churches, schools, and missionary societies" around the world.[30] Mr. Yale had been born in Boston but was uprooted to England when he was three. He donated books and other valuable resources to the Congregationalists of Connecticut. Because of this endowment, the Connecticut school was named for him. Yale is still sometimes called "Old Eli" in his honor.

> *"Where there is no religion, there is no morality . . . With the loss of religion . . . the ultimate foundation of confidence is blown up; and the security of life, liberty and property are buried in ruins."*
>
> Timothy Dwight,
> President of Yale, 1798

In the early years of Yale, the Word of God was preeminent. Consider, for example, the regulations for Yale College in its new charter in 1745. Here are two of the requirements listed: "All scholars shall live religious, godly, and blameless lives according to the rules of God's Word, diligently reading the Holy Scriptures, the fountain of light and truth; and constantly attend upon all the duties of religion, both in public and secret."[31] Furthermore, there was a penalty imposed for denying the faith: "If any scholar shall deny the Holy Scriptures or any part of them to be the Word of God, or be guilty of heresy or any error directly tending to subvert the fundamentals of Christianity, and continuing obstinate therein after the first and second admonition, he shall be expelled."[32]

One of the great presidents of Yale was a Godly man named Timothy Dwight (1752-1817). A grandson of Jonathan Edwards, Dwight helped spark a spiritual revival on campus. Many students accepted Jesus Christ, and a large percentage of them entered the ministry through Dwight's influence.

One can still find a remnant of believers at Yale today. There are even some professors who believe in Jesus, although they are certainly in the minority. About 1830, conflicts between the doctrines of Calvinism and Arminianism led to the decision that there would no longer be any doctrinal requirement to enter the school. That loosening of standards eventually led to Yale's losing its Christian distinctive entirely. That fact was first publicized by the young William F. Buckley, Jr., freshly graduated from Yale in the early 1950s, who wrote an exposé on the demise of Christianity at that school, entitled *God and Man at Yale.*

Columbia University

Another great Christian school in early America was Columbia University, founded in New York City in 1754. The original name was King's College to honor King George II, but the school was renamed in 1784.

An early advertisement for King's College read: "The chief thing that is aimed at in this college is to teach and engage children to know God in Jesus Christ."[33]

One of the delegates and signers of our Constitution, William Samuel Johnson from Connecticut, later served as the president of Columbia College. The sermon he preached to one of the graduating classes after the Revolutionary War gives us an indication of just how Christian Columbia was at that time:

> *"Without religion, I believe that learning does real mischief to the morals and principles of mankind."*
>
> Benjamin Rush, Signer of the Declaration of Independence

You this day, gentlemen, assume new characters, enter into new relations, and consequently incur new duties. You have, by the favor of Providence and the attention of friends, received a public education, the purpose whereof hath been to qualify you the better to serve your Creator and your country.

. . . .

Your first great duties, you are sensible, are those you owe to Heaven, to your Creator and Redeemer. Let these be ever present to your minds, and exemplified in your lives and conduct.

Imprint deep upon your minds the principles of piety towards God, and a reverence and fear of His holy name. The fear of God is the beginning of wisdom and its consummation is everlasting felicity. Possess yourselves of just and elevated notions of the Divine character, attributes, and administration, and of the end and dignity of your own immortal nature as it stands related to Him.

Reflect deeply and often upon those relations. Remember that it is in God you live and move and have your being, – that in the language of David He is about your bed and about your path and spieth out all your ways, – that there is not a thought in your hearts, nor a word upon your tongues, but lo! He knoweth them altogether, and that he will one day call you to a strict account for all your conduct in this mortal life.

Remember, too, that you are the redeemed of the Lord, that you are bought with a price, even the inestimable price of the precious blood of the Son of God. Adore Jehovah, therefore, as your God and your Judge. Love, fear, and serve Him as your Creator, Redeemer, and Sanctifier. Acquaint yourselves with Him in His word and holy ordinances.

Make Him your friend and protector and your felicity is secured both here and hereafter. And with respect to particular duties to Him, it is your happiness that you are well assured that he best serves his Maker, who does most good to his country and to mankind.[34]

> *"Under God's Power She Flourishes"*
>
> Princeton University's official motto

If you are a reader familiar with the Bible, you can hear this representative to our Constitutional Convention quoting or echoing many verses of Scripture to his students at Columbia University. It is unlikely this graduation sermon would be preached there today.

Princeton

Princeton was founded in the 18th century (in 1746) and did not become a liberal school until the early decades of the 20th century. For quite a few centuries, Princeton was a stalwart Christian institution.

Rev. Jonathan Dickinson was the first president of the College of New Jersey, which later became known as Princeton. Dickinson once said: "Cursed be all that learning that is contrary to the cross of Christ."[35]

One of the greatest presidents of Princeton was the worthy Christian patriot, Rev. John Witherspoon. He was the only active minister who signed the Declaration of Independence, although about two dozen of the signers had some seminary training. Dr. John Eidsmoe points out that Witherspoon was a man who greatly multiplied his influence on America: "John Witherspoon is best described as the man who shaped the men who shaped America. Although he did not attend the [1787] Constitutional Convention, his influence was multiplied many times over by those who spoke as well as by what was said."[36] It was said of Witherspoon that he was "as high a Son of Liberty as any man in America."[37]

New Jersey elected John Witherspoon to the Continental Congress that drafted the Declaration of Independence. When Congress called for a national day of fasting and prayer on May 17, 1776, John Witherspoon was called upon to preach the sermon. His topic was "The Dominion of Providence over the Affairs of Men."[38]

Witherspoon, as a delegate from New Jersey, played a key role in getting the Congress to approve the Declaration of Independence and is credited with delivering these famous words to his fellow delegates:

> There is a tide in the affairs of men. . . . We perceive it now before us. To hesitate is to consent to our own slavery. That noble instrument [the Declaration] should be subscribed to this very morning by every pen in this house. Though these gray hairs must soon descend to the sepulchre, I would infinitely rather that they descend thither by the hand of the executioner than desert at this crisis the sacred cause of my country.[39]

"It is in the man of piety and inward principle, that we may expect to find the uncorrupted patriot, the useful citizen, and the invincible soldier."

Rev. John Witherspoon, President of Princeton; signer of the Declaration of Independence

Later, during the war, Witherspoon and Princeton paid a price for their stand as British troops singled out this school as one of the targets for their cannon. Witherspoon's beloved library and other buildings went up in flames; but he believed that was a small price, which he was willing to pay, for liberty.

Some of the greatest theological minds in America have taught at Princeton, including Jonathan Edwards, Charles Hodge and his father, A. A. Hodge, and in the early part of the 20th century, B. B. Warfield. Unfortunately, none of these great men could likely obtain a position at Princeton today because their views are too conservative.

A University for Evangelizing the Indians

One early Ivy League school was founded entirely to raise up ministers and missionaries to the Indians. That school was Dartmouth in Hanover, New Hampshire. A Congregational minister, Eleazor Wheelock, founded the school in 1750 as Moor's Indian Charity School, and it was initially located in Lebanon, Connecticut.[40]

Conclusion

Modern secular educational philosophy is based on the theory that the primary responsibility for educating children rests with the state, not with the parents, but the Bible teaches something very different. God has given parents and churches, not the government, the responsibility for teaching children.

All education promotes someone's religion or lack thereof. Either teaching is done from the perspective that there is a God, that the Bible is His Holy Word, and that it can be relied upon as authoritative truth; or else teaching is done from the secular perspective that there is no God, that the Bible is not His Holy Word, and that nothing can be relied upon as authoritative truth. Both of these positions are religious viewpoints – either theistic or atheistic.

> *"You do well to wish to learn our arts and ways of life, and above all, the religion of Jesus Christ."*
>
> George Washington
> to the Delaware Indian chiefs

When modern judges and bureaucrats promote a secular public education, or attempt to shut down church schools that use a Bible curriculum, or try to hamstring the homeschool movement – they are making a religious choice, whether they acknowledge it or not. Too often the public schools of today have become "religion-free zones." Recent court decisions have gone to ridiculous lengths to keep any kind of religious – or perhaps we should say *Christian* – expression out of the public schools.

In this chapter we have learned that colonial children were taught to read by using the great theological truths of the Bible, Ivy League college presidents taught and preached the Gospel. One Ivy League college was completely devoted to training ministers to evangelize the Indians.

The American public school system was developed in 17th century Massachusetts so that children could learn to read the Bible. Virtually all the great colleges and universities of America were founded by Christians for Christian purposes. The Founding Fathers were imbued at these schools with a thoroughly Christian world-and-life-view that later permeated their politics.

So, the next time someone says that Christianity was not important to our Founding Fathers, remember the fifth thing every Christian should know about the founding of America – virtually all the settlers and founders of this great nation received a thoroughly Christian education, at the lower levels and, for those who attended, at the college level as well.

Chapter 6
The Great Awakening

*"The wind bloweth where it listeth, and thou hearest the sound thereof, but canst not
tell whence it cometh, and whither it goeth: so is every one that is born of the Spirit."*
~ John 3:8

**A religious revival was the key factor in uniting
the separate pre-Revolutionary War colonies.**

The Great Awakening was a spiritual movement, not a political one, but
it had political consequences as communications were established
between the various colonies up and down the eastern seaboard. Paul
Johnson says it was "the original dynamic of the continental movement for
independence."[1] The sixth thing every Christian should know about the
founding of America is that The Great Awakening, a religious revival, was a key
factor in uniting the separate pre-Revolutionary War colonies and in increasing
communication among them.

For about the first hundred and fifty years of their history, the separate
colonies of America were generally not in touch with one another, although each
was individually in touch with Mother England. Any border disputes or conflicts
over colonial charters were resolved back in the home country.

One exception to this general rule was the New England Confederation of
1643, which was comprised of four separate Puritan colonies in Massachusetts
and Connecticut. These colonies had united to form a league for their mutual
safety; and in drafting their mutual agreement, they again stated the reason they

had all come to these shores: "[W]e all came to these parts of America, with one and the same end and aim, namely, to advance the Kingdom of our Lord Jesus Christ."[2]

The other east coast colonies had little contact with each other until the mid-18th century, following the widespread spiritual revival known as the Great Awakening. The man who first advanced this inter-colonial communication was George Whitefield, the major evangelist of the Great Awakening and the first man to regularly travel up and down the east coast, visiting all thirteen colonies. This spiritual movement, with its accompanying development of inter-colonial lines of communication, played a significant role in paving the way for American independence. British historian Paul Johnson, author of *A History of the American People*, reports that the Great Awakening may have touched as many as three out of four American colonists.[3]

> *"Nothing can be more agreeable to the God of Peace than to see universal harmony and benevolence prevail among His creatures..."*
>
> Rev. Samuel Davies, Great Awakening preacher, "The Curse of Cowardice," 1758

The Great Awakening spiritually united all thirteen colonies in preparation for the Revolutionary War. Johnson says about that move of God's Spirit:

As we have seen, America had been founded primarily for religious purposes, and the Great Awakening had been the original dynamic of the continental movement for independence. The Americans were overwhelmingly church-going, much more so than the English, whose rule they rejected.[4]

In this chapter we will explore the indirect effect of the Great Awakening as a prelude to American independence. The American colonists tried very hard during the 1760s and 1770s to avoid a clash with Great Britain; but the king's arrogance and the arrogance of the House of Lords, along with other factors, such as the Crown's attempt to control colonial commerce and the colonists' fear that the Church of England would be imposed as the colonial state church, propelled the colonies toward independence. Christianity ultimately played a large role in a united effort to become free from Mother England.

The Work of the Holy Spirit

There are special times in the life of a person when the Holy Spirit does extraordinary work, when a person is convicted of sin and drawn into the Kingdom. There are also times in the life of a nation when God does a mighty work, times when the people cry out as on the day of Pentecost: "What must we do to be saved?"

Many people have tried to analyze how a revival gets started and what the conditions should be for true repentance to take place. Jesus compared the Holy Spirit to the wind. We can hear it, feel it, and see its effect; but there seems to be absolutely no way we can control it. Revival is the work of the sovereign Spirit of God. It happens where and when He wills it.

In the middle of the 1700s a sovereign move of God occurred in colonial America. It happened when the country was still unformed, before the new nation was born. It was the Great Awakening, in large measure, that determined the kind of Christian nation America would become.

> "[The Great Awakening] was indeed one of the key events in American history."
>
> Paul Johnson

It is hard to specifically define when the Great Awakening began and when it ended, but it was definitely ongoing in the early and mid-eighteenth century. The height of the revival occurred between 1730 and 1770. Several preachers were involved, but two names stand out – Jonathan Edwards from New England and George Whitefield from Old England. From Massachusetts, this revival spread to New Hampshire and Connecticut; it went through the Middle colonies – New York, New Jersey, Pennsylvania, and Delaware – and by 1740, it had also reached the South.

A Rural Beginning

The Great Awakening touched the rural areas as well as the big cities. It cut across denominational lines, and broke any remaining strongholds of the Church of England. When individual Christians began to make independent decisions about what to believe and where to worship, a democratic spirit was created that helped lay the foundation for the American Revolution.

The Great Awakening was a movement with great personal, social, and political consequences. Yet, the message delivered by its preachers was simply the truth of the Bible – especially regarding the nature of Man, his need for salvation, and the consequences of a changed heart leading to a Godly life of service.

According to Paul Johnson, the Great Awakening had its early roots among German immigrants who were most thankful for this "promised land" and for their delivery from poverty in Germany. Johnson writes:

> In 1719 the German pastor of the Dutch Reformed Church, Theodore Frelinghuysen, led a series of revival meetings in the Raritan Valley [in New Jersey]. "Pietism," the emphasis on leading a holy life without troubling too much about the doctrinal disputes which racked the 17th century, was a German concept, and this is the first time we find non-English-speaking immigrants bringing with them ideas which influenced American intellectual life.[5]

Another early preacher of the Great Awakening was a Scotch-Irish Presbyterian named William Tennent (1673-1745) who made Neshaminy, Pennsylvania, his new home. He established the Log College, which later became the College of New Jersey and, ultimately, the great college of Princeton. Both he and his son Gilbert were fiery preachers who practiced what Paul Johnson calls "Frontier Religion" with emotional hymn-singing. They emphasized Godly living and the need for personal Bible study. The requirement for personal Bible study made reading – and therefore, education – a must.

> *"God made it, I suppose, the greatest occasion of awakening to others, of anything that ever came to pass in the town [Northampton, Mass.]."*
>
> Jonathan Edwards,
> *Narrative of Surprising Conversions*

This linkage of the knowledge of God with knowledge in general and the need for Bible reading caused the literacy rate among the white population in America to climb to nearly 100% in the late 1700s. Paul Johnson notes the Tennents' impact on Christian higher education: "Many of Tennent's pupils, or disciples, became prominent preachers themselves, all over the colonies, and his Log College became the prototype for the famous College of New Jersey, founded in 1746, which eventually settled at Princeton."[6] Jonathan Edwards, another prominent preacher of the Great Awakening, would one day become president of Princeton.

Jonathan Edwards

Jonathan Edwards (1703-1758) was one of the greatest minds America ever produced. It was his fire and brimstone messages, his pleading for sinners to repent while there was still time, and his word pictures of God's love and kindness that drew people by the thousands into the Kingdom. Although he is perhaps best known for his sermon "Sinners in the Hands of an Angry God," Edwards generally preached the love of God more than His judgment.

Jonathan Edwards was the third president of Princeton, which at the time was still known as the College of New Jersey. Edwards had a brilliant mind and wrote his first theological paper at the age of ten. A philosopher as well as a theologian, Edwards was a Puritan Congregationalist, and his view of Christianity as an equalizer of people helped pave the way for the American Revolution. He once said: "There is no leveler like Christianity, but it levels by lifting all who receive it to the lofty table-land of a true character and of undying hope both for this world and the next."[7]

Jonathan Edwards' influence reached far beyond his time. Not only were thousands converted through his sermons, both heard and read; but even the unconverted benefited from the social and political consequences of his preaching. He and his wife Sara (Sara Pierrepont, whom he married in 1727) had eleven children who were all raised to be Godly people. William J. Federer notes:

> Their success as parents was revealed in a study done in 1990, showing that their descendants included 13 college presidents, 65 professors, 30 judges, 100 lawyers, a dean of a prestigious law school, 80 public office holders, nearly 100 missionaries, 3 mayors of large cities, 3 governors, 3 United States Senators, 1 comptroller of the United States Treasury and 1 Vice-President of the United States.[8]

Most of these men and women were as Godly as their ancestors had been; but tragically, the last person listed, Vice President Aaron Burr, lived a life in rebellion to the Christianity of his childhood. Aaron Burr was a man of low character who killed Alexander Hamilton in a duel. Later Burr would be rightfully accused of treason. Burr had tragically abandoned the Christianity of his famous grandfather; but thankfully, he was the exception, not the rule, in Jonathan Edwards' extended family of Christian civil servants.

In his book, *Men Who Shaped America,* author Robert Flood tells how Jonathan Edwards faithfully preached at the Congregational church at Northampton, Massachusetts week in and week out – at first, with little result. But then God moved in a great way – despite the fact that Edwards was near-sighted and delivered his sermons by reading them in a dull monotone.

Flood writes: "Then revival began in 1734 while Jonathan Edwards was preaching a series of sermons on justification by faith alone. Conversions began, first the young, then their elders. A notorious young woman was saved. It was like a 'flash of lightning' to the young people."[9]

Edwards himself describes the events of the following year: "In the spring and summer following, anno 1735, the town seemed to be full of the presence of God; it never was so full of love, nor of joy, and yet so full of distress, as it was then."[10] The distress was a sign of repentance and agonizing over sin.

Edwards documented the beginning of this revival in his book, *A Faithful Narrative on the Surprising Work of God in the Conversion of Many Hundred Souls in Northampton.* Here is a sampling of that book's first-hand accounting of events:

> And then it was, in the latter part of December, that the Spirit of God began extraordinarily to . . . work amongst us. There were, very suddenly, one after another, five or six persons who were, to all appearance, savingly converted, and some of them wrought upon in a very remarkable manner.
>
> Particularly I was surprised with the relation of a young woman, who had been one of the greatest company-keepers in the whole town. When she came to me, I had never heard that she was become in any ways serious, but by the conversation I had with her, it appeared to me that what she gave an account of was a glorious work of God's infinite power and sovereign grace, and that God had given her a new heart, truly broken and sanctified.
>
> . . . .
>
> God made it, I suppose, the greatest occasion of awakening to others, of anything that ever came to pass in the town. I have had abundant opportunity to know the effect it had, by my private conversation with many. The news of it seemed to be almost like a flash of lighting upon the hearts of young people all over the town, and upon many others.
>
> . . . .
>
> Presently upon this, a great and earnest concern about the great things of religion and the eternal world became universal in all parts of the town and among persons of all degrees and all ages. The noise of the dry bones waxed louder and louder.
>
> . . . .
>
> Those that were wont to be the vainest and loosest, and those that had been the most disposed to think and speak slightly of vital and experimental religion, were not generally subject to great awakenings. And the work of conversion was carried on in a most astonishing manner and increased more and more; souls did, as it were, come by flocks to Jesus Christ.
>
> . . . .

This work of God, as it was carried on and the number of true saints multiplied, soon made a glorious alteration in the town . . . there were remarkable tokens of God's presence in almost every house. It was a time of joy in families on the account of salvation's being brought unto them, parents rejoicing over their children as new born, and husbands over their wives, and wives over their husbands.

The goings of God were then seen in His sanctuary, God's day was a delight and His tabernacles were amiable. Our public assembles were then beautiful; the congregation was alive in God's service, everyone earnestly intent on the public worship, every hearer eager to drink the words of the minister as they came from his mouth.

The assembly in general were, from time to time, in tears while the word was preached, some weeping with sorrow and distress, others with joy and love, others with pity and concern for their neighbors.

There were many instances of persons that came from abroad, on visits or on business . . . [that] partook of that shower of divine blessing that God rained down here and went home rejoicing. Till at length the same work began to appear and prevail in several other towns in the country[11]

To this point in his narrative, Edwards had been describing the revival that took place in Northampton, which is closer in proximity to Hartford than it is to Boston. He next describes this move of God as it began to spread to other areas. Edwards continues:

In the month of March, the people of South Hadley began to be seized with a deep concern about the things of religion, which very soon became universal . . . About the same time, it began to break forth in the west part of Suffield . . . and it soon spread into all parts of the town.

It next appeared at Sunderland. . . . About the same time it began to appear in a part of Deerfield . . . Hatfield . . . West Springfield . . . Long Meadow . . . Endfield . . . Westfield . . . Northfield. . . . In every place, God brought His saving blessings with Him, and His Word, attended with Spirit . . . returned not void.[12]

At the height of the Great Awakening, the New England churches grew daily. Robert Flood reports that between 1740 and 1742, out of a total population of 300,000 souls in New England, 25,000 to 50,000 people joined the churches. "The movement changed the entire moral tone of New England for the better and justly earned the name of a 'Great Awakening.'"[13]

Today when high school children study about the Great Awakening, and perhaps even read excerpts from "Sinners in the Hands of an Angry God," they generally discuss how strange and distant the Puritans' views seem from our own, but God was using His humble servant, Jonathan Edwards, to prepare the hearts of the people to become a great nation.

George Whitefield

The other famous preacher of the Great Awakening was George Whitefield (1714-1770). Like Jonathan Edwards, he was a committed Calvinist. Whitefield came from Old England, where he had attended Oxford University with John and Charles Wesley, brothers who were great British evangelists and hymn-writers.

> "Joy — joy unspeakable — joy that's full of grace, big with glory!"
>
> George Whitefield
> at the time of his Conversion,
> 1733

After Whitefield's conversion, he preached salvation to the lost – within the English churches. As his message appeared to be more and more directed against the established church, he was forced to preach outside and soon was preaching to thousands and tens of thousands. Flood writes of Whitefield: "At Bristol, England, he had preached to 20,000 at one gathering and all could hear. In America he preached to 5,000 on Boston Common and to 8,000 at one time in the fields. And even at Harvard they received him well, though some held doubts."[14]

The Lord used Whitefield to start a fire of revival throughout the colonies. Paul Johnson describes this phenomenon:

> He simply carried a torch and used it to set alight multitudes. He found America greatly to his taste. In 1740 he made the first continental tour of the colonies, from Savannah in Georgia to Boston in the north, igniting violent sheets of religious flame everywhere. It was Whitefield, the Grand Itinerant as he was known, who caused the Great Awakening to take off.[15]

Rev. Whitefield came to Philadelphia, where Benjamin Franklin heard him preach and even printed many of his sermons. Although Franklin did not agree with Whitefield's views, he seems to have been fascinated with his preaching, which clearly had a strong impact on the hearers. Ben Franklin was fascinated with this gifted evangelist, and offered this description of him:

> In 1739 arrived among us from Ireland the Reverend Mr. Whitefield, who had made himself remarkable there as an itinerant preacher. He was at first permitted to preach in some of our churches; but the clergy, taking a dislike to him, soon refused him their pulpits, and he was obliged to preach in the fields. The multitudes of all sects and denominations that attended his sermons were enormous, and it was a matter of speculation to me, who was one of the number, to observe the extraordinary influence of his oratory on his hearers, and how much they admired and respected him, notwithstanding his common abuse of them, by assuring them they were naturally *half beasts and half devils.*[16]

George Whitefield preached from New England to Georgia, uniting all the colonies spiritually before American independence was even a dream.

One of Whitefield's great works of charity was located in the southernmost British-American colony of Georgia. Many parents had died there under the harsh conditions of clearing the land, leaving a great number of "helpless children unprovided for," said Ben Franklin. He then tells how George Whitefield's heart was touched to found an orphanage for their support and education.

One of Whitefield's aims in his itinerant preaching during the Great Awakening was to raise money for this "Orphan House." Although the evangelist's enemies suspected (without cause) that Whitefield may have squandered some of the money for personal purposes, Ben Franklin disagreed:

> *"In some places, thousands cried out aloud; many as in the agonies of death; most were drowned in tears; some turned pale as death; others were wringing their hands; others lying on the ground; others sinking into the arms of their friends; almost all lifting up their eyes, and calling for mercy."*
>
> John Wesley on the impact of the ministry of George Whitefield

> Some of Mr. Whitefield's enemies affected to suppose that he would apply these collections to his own private emolument; but I, who was intimately acquainted with him (being employed in printing his Sermons and Journals, etc.), never had the least suspicion of his integrity, but am to this day decidedly of opinion that he was in all his conduct a perfectly *honest man;* and methinks

my testimony in his favour ought to have the more weight, as we had no religious connection. He used, indeed, sometimes to pray for my conversion, but never had the satisfaction of believing that his prayers were heard. Ours was a mere civil friendship, sincere on both sides, and lasted to his death.[17]

Franklin continues with a first-hand account of the natural gifts bestowed on this great preacher of the Great Awakening:

He had a loud and clear voice, and articulated his words so perfectly, that he might be heard and understood at a great distance, especially as his auditors, however numerous, observed the most exact silence . . . I computed that he might well be heard by more than thirty thousand [in Philadelphia]."[18]

> "... *Except a man be born again, he cannot see the kingdom of God"*
> *(John 3:3b)*
>
> The Scriptural Text of
> 300 Sermons by
> George Whitefield

The chief message delivered by George Whitefield was "you must be born again." Someone once asked him why he stressed that theme so much.

"Why do you always preach that you must be born again?"

The great preacher replied: "Because you *must* be born again."

George Whitefield also preached about new life in Christ. For example, in one of his sermons he declared:

Never rest until you can say, "the Lord our righteousness." Who knows but the Lord may have mercy, nay, abundantly pardon you? Beg of God to give you faith; and if the Lord give you that, you will by it receive Christ, with his righteousness, and his all.
. . . .
None, none can tell, but those happy souls who have experienced it with what demonstration of the Spirit this conviction comes. . . . Oh, how amiable, as well as all sufficient, does the blessed Jesus now appear! With what new eyes does the soul now see the Lord its righteousness! Brethren, it is unutterable.
. . . .
Those who live godly in Christ, may not so much be said to live, as Christ to live in them. . . . They are led by the Spirit as a child is led by the hand of its father.
. . . .
They hear, know, and obey his voice. . . . Being born again in God they

habitually live to, and daily walk with God.[19]

Sarah Edwards, Jonathan's wife, said this about the impact of George Whitefield's messages: "It is wonderful to see what a spell he casts over an audience by proclaiming the simplest truths of the Bible. . . . Our mechanics shut up their shops, and the day laborers throw down their tools to go and hear him preach, and few return unaffected."[20]

Whitefield returned repeatedly to America. Paul Johnson writes: "[H]e returned again and again to the attack – seven continental tours in the thirty years from 1740 – and all churches benefited from his efforts, though the greatest gainers were the Baptists and the stranger sects on the Protestant fringes."[21]

Even Ben Franklin commented on the social effects of the revival and of Whitefield's preaching:

> It was wonderful to see the change soon made in the manners of our inhabitants. From being thoughtless or indifferent about religion, it seemed as if all the world were growing religious, so that one could not walk through the town in an evening without hearing psalms sung in different families of every street.[22]

Whitefield had a special place in his heart for America. He died near Boston in 1770 only a few hours after preaching his last sermon. According to Russell Hitt: "[H]e dared to trust that his preaching might help create one nation under God – thirteen scattered colonies united with each other."[23]

The Death-Knell of British Colonialism
An important side benefit of the Great Awakening was that it paved the way for the founding of the United States of America. Paul Johnson points out that this Great Awakening "sounded the death-knell of British colonialism."[24]

The Great Awakening helped to forge all sections of the country together. Dr. Ellis Sandoz of Louisiana State University points out:

> The denominational differences are minimized partly as a result of the homogenizing and democratizing effects of decades of revivalism from the Great Awakening and its rumbling echoes and aftershocks. That the leading lights of the Revolutionary Congresses and the Federal Convention were generally men of faith can no longer be doubted.[25]

The thirteen colonies had already been united spiritually by the 1770s when the British Parliament, along with the king, passed a series of legislative acts to unreasonably tax, subdue, and control the American colonists in Boston. Therefore, it seemed reasonable that all of the other colonies should come to the aid of their Boston brethren.

One of those vexing British measures was the Port Act of 1774, closing the harbor of that most rebellious American city, Boston – which had been the site of the Boston Tea Party in December 1773. What the British did not count on was that other colonists would come to the aid of the Bostonians.

In fact, the British actively tried to discourage other colonies from helping Boston by publishing lies about their interest in this matter. Bancroft points out:

> It was published at the corners of the streets that Pennsylvania would refuse to suspend commerce; that the society of Friends [the Quakers] would arrest every step toward war; that New York would never name deputies to a congress; that the power of Great Britain could not fail to crush resistance.[26]

But on June 1, 1774, at midnight, the Port Act went into effect as scheduled and British ships converged into Boston Harbor to begin an indefinite blockade. George Bancroft describes the somber response from two other American colonies: "At Philadelphia, the bells of the churches were muffled and tolled, the ships in port hoisted their colors at half mast. . . . In Virginia, the population thronged the churches; Washington attended the service and strictly kept the fast."[27] George Washington's diary entry for June 1, 1774 reads: "Went to church and fasted all day."[28]

Great Britain had thrown down the gauntlet, but the colonies were now united. If the British thought they were picking a fight only with Boston, they were badly mistaken.

All the colonies were moved to help Boston or at least to sympathize with that city. It took only three weeks for the American Continental Congress to reprimand General Thomas Gage, the British military leader responsible for closing the harbor. Congress accused him of engaging in behavior tending "to involve a free people in the horrors of war."[29]

The people of Boston received more than moral support from the other colonies. South Carolina was the first to respond with two hundred barrels of rice. Throughout New England, towns sent grain, peas, oil, fish, livestock, and money to help the people of Boston. The people of Norfolk sent a letter of support, reassuring the Bostonians: "Our hearts are warmed with affection for you . . . we address the Almighty Ruler to support you in your afflictions; be assured we consider you as suffering in the common cause, and look upon ourselves as bound by the most sacred ties to support you."[30]

The king's plans for subduing the colonies were not limited to Massachusetts. The colonists feared that with the passage of the Regulating Act in 1774, King George and the Parliament wanted to impose the Anglican Church as the state church on the whole of America.[31] If that happened, the whole Puritan "errand into the wilderness," as well as the experiments in religious liberty in all the colonies, would be extinguished after a hundred and fifty years of freedom earned at the expense of blood, sweat, and toil.

George Bancroft points out how serious the new Regulating Act was: "Without previous notice to Massachusetts and without a hearing, it took away rights and liberties which the people had enjoyed from the foundation of the colony."[32]

Although some colonists continued to be Loyalists and support the British, many gradually began to realize that the freedoms their forefathers had sacrificed so much for were about to be lost. William Prescott of Pepperell, Massachusetts, reflected the thinking of those colonists who favored independence:

> We think, if we submit to these regulations, all is gone. Our forefathers passed the vast Atlantic, spent their blood and treasure that they might enjoy their liberties, both civil and religious, and transmit them to their posterity. Their children have waded through seas of difficulty, to leave us free and happy in the enjoyment of English privileges. Now, if we should give them up, can our children rise up and call us blessed? Is a glorious death in defense of our liberties better than a short infamous life, and our memories to be had in detestation to the latest posterity?[33]

Even the British Loyalist, General Gage, wrote to the king and suggested that this Regulating Act, revoking the charter of Massachusetts with its accompanying subjection to arbitrary British control, was too much for the colonists to bear and that Boston had friends up and down the American coast. He suggested that such measures be overturned. But the king was not moved, declaring, "The New England governments are now in a state of rebellion; blows must decide whether they are to be subject to this country or to be independent."[34]

When Ben Franklin heard of the king's response, he told his closest associates that the only real safety for America would be as a free country. William Lisle Bowles said to Edmund Burke, one of the few British statesmen to oppose the war against America: "The cause of freedom is the cause of God."[35]

These conflicts were later reflected in the Declaration of Independence when Thomas Jefferson listed more than twenty-eight specific complaints against the King of England. One of these complaints alluded to the Regulating Act: "For taking away our charters, abolishing our most valuable laws, and altering fundamentally the forms of our governments . . ."[36]

Conclusion

Paul Johnson, who has been quoted a great deal in this chapter, pointed out that the message of the Great Awakening, which created new men and women in Christ in all thirteen colonies, had "undoubted political undertones."[37] He concludes: "The Great Awakening was thus the proto-revolutionary event, the formative movement in American history, preceding the political drive for independence, and making it possible."[38]

The key text for the Great Awakening was Revelation 21:5: "Behold, I make all things new." Johnson also describes this verse as "the text for the American experience as a whole."[39]

The colonists had no intention of permitting their liberties to be lost. They immediately rallied around Boston, now their spiritual cousin as well as their neighbor, as soon as the king began to threaten the liberty of that colony.

Paul Johnson shares the thoughts of President John Adams on the link between the Great Awakening and the founding of America:

> As John Adams was to put it, long afterwards: "The Revolution was effected before the War commenced. The Revolution was in the mind and hearts of the people: and change in their religious sentiments of their duties and obligations." . . . The Revolution could not have taken place without this religious background. The essential difference between the American Revolution and the French Revolution is that the American Revolution, in its origins, was a religious event, whereas the French Revolution was an anti-religious event.[40]

The sixth thing every Christian should know about the founding of America is that it was the religious revival of the Great Awakening that fired the American Revolution and set it on a successful course. God was continuing to superintend His plantings in the wilderness of America.

Chapter 7
The Black Regiment

"... take away your exactions from my people, saith the Lord God."
~ Ezekiel 45:9b

Many of the clergy in the American colonies, members of the Black Regiment, "preached liberty."

The colonial pulpit was a major source of strength and inspiration both before and during the Revolutionary War for Independence. In particular, the ministers of New England played a pivotal role in calling for independence and for Godly resistance to British tyranny. At least twice a year, and always around the time of local election days, the clergy would preach an election sermon on the state of political affairs.

The seventh thing every Christian should know about the founding of America is that many of the clergy in the American colonies "preached liberty."[1] The pulpits of New England were especially important in helping to bring about independence. Long before the general population understood the threat to American liberty, some colonial ministers saw what was coming and boldly spoke out about it from their pulpits.

Because of the color of their robes, these patriotic clergy were known as the Black Regiment. Other colonials, who were organized to protect their towns from the British at a moment's notice, were called Minutemen. They were generally laymen from a particular local church, led by their minister or deacon who conducted military drills after Sunday services. Rev. Jonas Clark is a good example of the Black Regiment. He was in charge of the Minutemen in Lexington who were attacked in the first conflict of the Revolutionary War.

The Puritan Pulpits

Another example of the Black Regiment was Dr. Samuel Cooper, minister of the Brattle Street Church in Boston. He was a friend of Samuel Adams, Benjamin Franklin, and John Adams. One of his faithful parishioners was John Hancock. Like so many in the Black Regiment, he was a Harvard graduate.

Dr. Cooper summarized the sentiments of the Black Regiment when he echoed Jeremiah 6:14 in his election sermon at Boston in 1780 during the War: "Peace, peace, we ardently wish; but not upon terms dishonorable to ourselves, or dangerous to our liberties; and our enemies seem not yet prepared to allow it upon any other."[2]

> *"The prominence of ministers in the political literature of the period attests to the continuing influence of religion during the founding era."*
>
> Dr. Donald S. Lutz,
> political science professor

George Bancroft describes these clergy patriots, whom he calls the "memorable divines" of New England, as a key to uniting their congregations in defense of liberty:

From the sermons of memorable divines, who were gone to a heavenly country, leaving their names precious among the people of God on earth, a brief collection of faithful testimonies to the cause of God and his New England people was circulated by the press, that the hearts of the rising generation might know what had been the great end of the plantations, and count it their duty and their glory to continue in those right ways of the Lord wherein their fathers walked before them.

Their successors in the ministry, all pupils of Harvard or Yale, true ministers to the people, unequaled in metaphysical acuteness and familiarity with the principles of political freedom, were heard as of old with reverence by their congregations in their meeting-houses on every Lord's day, and on special occasions of fasts, thanksgivings, lectures, and military musters. Elijah's mantle being caught up was a happy token that the Lord would be with this generation, as he had been with their fathers. Their exhaustless armory was the Bible, whose scriptures furnished sharp words to point their appeals, apt examples of resistance, prophetic denunciations of the enemies of God's people, and promises of the divine blessing on the defenders of his law.[3]

Two important concepts stand out in this description. For members of the Black Regiment, defending liberty was the same as defending God's law. Secondly, these sermons were published and circulated throughout the colonies in the press – greatly magnifying their impact.

Preaching Liberty

Many Americans understand that the very first settlers of New England were devout Christians. However, we are generally led to believe that, by the time of the founding era, whatever faith there had been was long since evaporated.

There is a nugget of truth in this analysis in the sense that as prosperity began to grow in the colonies, many second and third generation believers did abandon the faith, at least inwardly. George Whitefield had reported when he first visited Boston in 1740: "It has the form of religion kept up, but has lost much of its power."[4]

> *"The scriptures cannot rightly be expounded without explaining them in a manner friendly to the cause of freedom."*
>
> Rev. Charles Turner,
> Duxbury, Mass.

Secular historians often play down the role of the Great Awakening in preparing the colonists for independence. Probably for much the same reasons, they almost universally ignore the Black Regiment, those ministers up and down the American coast who played such a significant role in stirring the souls of the colonists to liberty.

Members of the Black Regiment had a great deal to say about the tyranny of the king and Parliament. Rev. Jonathan Mayhew, minister of West Church in Boston, preached a sermon in 1765 after learning of King George's Stamp Act, in which he declared that the king had thus forfeited his rightful authority over his American subjects. Rev. Mayhew reasoned:

> The king is as much bound by his oath not to infringe the legal rights of the people, as the people are bound to yield subjection to him. From whence it follows that as soon as the prince sets himself above the law, he loses the king in the tyrant. He does, to all intents and purposes, un-king himself.[5]

As far back as the Magna Carta in 1215 and the Glorious Revolution of

1688, with its subsequent Bill of Rights (1689), English citizens had extracted more rights from their monarchs than any other people on earth. The New England clergy were well aware of these rights and regularly reminded their congregations of them.

God's Intervention

Rev. Phillips Payson of Chelsea, Massachusetts, was another bold servant of God who led his laymen as Minutemen. There had been numerous times during the war effort when God Himself had seemed to intervene. About three years into the War for Independence, during a time when the hand of God was clearly favoring the Americans, General George Washington acknowledged that fact in a letter to fellow Virginian Thomas Nelson, Jr., one of the signers of the Declaration of Independence.

> "The road to American freedom was paved in large part by the pulpits of New England. Sermons from the colonial era helped to shape the American understanding that 'resistance to tyranny is obedience to God.'"
>
> D. James Kennedy and Jerry Newcombe, What If Jesus Had Never Been Born?

Washington pointed out in this letter, written on August 20, 1778: "The hand of Providence has been so conspicuous in all this, that he must be worse than an infidel that lacks faith, and more than wicked, that has not gratitude enough to acknowledge his obligations."[6]

In expressing these sentiments, the father of our country was echoing a message delivered earlier in 1778 by a member of the Black Regiment. Rev. Payson had preached in an election sermon in Boston: "We must be infidels, the worst of infidels, to disown or disregard the hand that has raised us up such benevolent and powerful assistants in times of great distress."[7] Both the clergyman and the General understood that the Americans were not fighting alone. It seemed obvious that God was on their side or rather that they were on God's side in the fight for liberty.

Watchmen on the Walls

Those clergy in the Black Regiment during the founding era can be likened to the watchmen on the wall described by the prophet in Ezekiel 3:17-21. The watchman would look down at all who were entering the gates of the walled city and warn the citizens if necessary. Rev. Franklin P. Cole, a modern-day pastor who studied at Oxford University, wrote about the New England clergy and the role they played in our War for Independence:

> The New England minister of the Revolutionary era was a watchman on
> several walls. He was a guardian of education. Practically all the Puritan clergy
> had been educated at Harvard or Yale; the most influential of them having their
> Master's or Doctor's degree. In 1764, of the fifty-two settled Congregational
> ministers in New Hampshire, forty-eight were college graduates.[8]

Rev. Cole points out that colonial ministers were generally well-rounded in
their studies, not merely learned in theology: "Contrary to popular opinion of the
present day, many of the ministers of the Revolutionary period were interested in
other fields of knowledge besides theology."[9]

In addition to quoting from and expounding on
the Bible, the Black Regiment would also sometimes
quote from John Locke, John Milton, Algernon
Sydney, Baron Montesquieu, and Samuel Butler.
Milton and Butler were Puritans. Locke wrote *The
Reasonableness of Christianity*. Sydney was a friend of
William Penn and a professing Christian who set
forth his governmental ideals in a treatise, *Discourses*

> *"The minister was
> usually the best
> educated man in his
> community."*
>
> Franklin Cole,
> *They Preached Liberty*

Concerning Government, that greatly influenced political thought in 18th century
America. The writings of Baron de Charles Louis de Secondat Montesquieu
contain many pro-Christian sentiments. For example, in his *The Spirit of Laws*,
Montesquieu wrote: "We shall see that we owe to Christianity, in government, a
certain political law, and in war a certain law of nations – benefits which human
nature can never sufficiently acknowledge."[10]

The Founding Fathers quoted from these same sources, and also quoted
frequently from Sir William Blackstone, an Englishman who documented the
Christian basis of British common law in his popular series of *Commentaries* on
British common law. Blackstone sold more of his *Commentaries* in the colonies
during the 1770s than he did in England.

Political science professor Donald S. Lutz, author of *The Origins of American
Constitutionalism*, discusses the major impact of the Bible on the decision to
separate from England:

> When reading comprehensively in the political literature of the war years, one
> cannot but be struck by the extent to which biblical sources used by ministers
> . . . undergirded the justification for the break with Britain, the rationale for

continuing the war, and the basic principles of Americans' writing their own constitutions.[11]

Election Day Sermons

Elections were held in most colonies, and certainly in New England, every year. This democratic practice was an outgrowth of the Reformation's emphasis on the sinfulness of man. Rev. Cole discusses the election sermons preached by the Black Regiment:

It was in the so-called "Election Sermons" of Massachusetts, Connecticut, New Hampshire, and Vermont that the ministers expressed themselves most fluently on the subject of civil government. According to the Rev. William Gordon of Roxbury, an historian of the Revolution: "Two sermons have been preached annually for a length of time, the one on general election day, the last Wednesday in May, when the new general court has been used to meet, according to charter, and elect counsellors for the ensuing year; the other, some little while after, on artillery election day, when the officers are re-elected, or new officers chosen. On these occasions political subjects are deemed very proper; but it is expected that they be treated in a decent, serious, and instructive manner. . . . The sermon is styled the *Election Sermon* and is printed. Every representative has a copy for himself, and generally one or more for the minister or ministers of his town. As the patriots have prevailed, the preachers of each sermon have been the zealous friends of liberty; and the passages most adapted to promote the spread and love of it have been selected and circulated far and wide by means of newspapers."[12]

> *"There is probably no group of men in history, living in a particular area at a given time, who can speak as forcibly on the subject of liberty as the Congregational ministers of New England between 1750 and 1785."*
>
> Franklin P. Cole

And, of course, the Scriptures were the source for these election sermons, which were then printed in the newspaper and given a wide circulation, thereby spreading the love of liberty drawn from the Bible. Today's newspapers would be more likely to report favorably on the political views of the latest "pop" singer or actress than of the local ministers.

No Fairweather Friends of Liberty

Rev. Cole makes the point that these ministers of the Black Regiment were friends of liberty both in season and out of season; they were patriots whether conditions were favorable or unfavorable. Such faithfulness was in stark contrast to some in the merchant class who were sometimes friends of liberty and sometimes friends of the British. Rev. Cole explains:

> With the powerful New England merchants the case was different. They were conscious of their liberties only when their prosperity was threatened. . . . When the Townshend Acts of 1767, laying duties on tea, lead, glass, etc., were passed, the merchants were vocal in their annoyance. But when the Acts were repealed, they were prepared to bury the hatchet with England, but to wield another against Sam Adams and his confederates who were "disturbing the peace." A few years later, however, when Lord North in 1773 granted the East India Company the monopoly on the transportation of tea to America, the merchants again stood with the "hundred percent patriots." Thus in the decade preceding the Revolution economic fortune or misfortune determined for the merchant class their convictions regarding political liberty.[13]

> *"Witness a great, if not the greatest, part of the known world, who are now groaning, but not murmuring, under the heavy yoke of tyranny!"*
>
> Rev. Jonathan Mayhew

In contrast to these merchants, the New England clergy were pro-freedom, come what may:

> They rejoiced with the lawyers and tradesmen when the Stamp Act was repealed; in fact, practically every pulpit rang with "the good news from a far land." . . . The ministers before and during the Revolution stood, with few exceptions, near the center of liberty's wall. They were, as a group, neither radical nor reactionary in their political philosophy.[14]

One Massachusetts clergyman, Abraham Keteltas, declared in 1777:

> The most precious remains of civil liberty the world can now boast of, are lodged in our hands. . . . [This war is] the cause of truth, against error and falsehood . . . the cause of pure and undefiled religion, against bigotry, superstition, and human inventions. . . . In short, it is the cause of heaven

against hell – of the kind Parent of the universe against the prince of darkness, and the destroyer of the human race.[15]

The Black Regiment was so powerful in 1774 before the War began that when the people of Massachusetts wanted their royalist pro-British governor, Thomas Hutchinson, to call for a day of fasting and prayer, he refused because he feared what might be said in the pulpits on such a day. He observed that "the request was only to give an opportunity for sedition to flow from the pulpit."[16]

Beyond New England

Although there were many in the Black Regiment from other colonies and other regions, it was the New England pulpit in particular to which this honorary title is given. These clergy were by far the most active in preaching liberty. But beyond New England, the Black Regiment had other faithful members like Rev. Sam Davies of Virginia. John Adams observed, "The Philadelphia ministers 'thunder and lighten every Sabbath' against George III's despotism."[17] And, in speaking of his native Virginia, Thomas Jefferson observed, "[P]ulpit oratory ran like a shock of electricity through the whole colony."[18]

Rev. Sam Davies, a minister in Hanover County, Virginia, preached a powerful sermon against cowardice during the War. He asked: "[I]s it not our duty, in the sight of God, is it not a work to which the Lord loudly calls us, to take up arms for the defense of our country?"[19]

Jonathan Mayhew

Rev. Jonathan Mayhew (1720-1766) was one of the most profound thinkers in the Black Regiment and one of the greatest New England friends of liberty. He was a graduate of Harvard and served West Church in Boston from 1747 until his death in 1766, a full decade before the Declaration of Independence was written.

Rev. Mayhew was the quintessential clergyman of the Black Regiment. Early on, he saw the inevitability of American independence for righteousness' sake. He preached against British tyranny as a sin from which the people under its oppression had an obligation to rebel. For example:

> The people know for what end they set up, and maintain, their governors; and they are the proper judges when they execute their trust as they ought to do it;
> – when their prince exercises an equitable and paternal authority over them; –

when from a prince and common father, he exalts himself into a tyrant – when from subjects and children, he degrades them into the class of slaves; – plunders them, makes them his prey, and unnaturally sports himself with their lives and fortunes.[20]

Rev. Mayhew knew that the power of government was invested in the people. He also knew that the consent of the governed was more important than the petty whims of magistrates who lose their authority to rule over the people when they become tyrants. Such radical preaching played a major role in the drive for independence. Franklin Cole regrets that Rev. Mayhew in little known in America today:

It is regrettable that Jonathan Mayhew is not better known and more rightfully honored by our generation. For he was an inspired, courageous pioneer, not only in his theological thought, but also in his convictions regarding civil and religious liberties. Robert Treat Paine, a signer of the Declaration of Independence and one-time attorney-general of the United States, called Mayhew "The Father of Civil and Religious Liberty in Massachusetts and America."[21]

> *"And while I am speaking of loyalty to our earthly Prince, suffer me just to put you in mind to be loyal also to the supreme RULER of the universe, by whom kings reign, and princes decree justice."*
>
> Rev. Jonathan Mayhew

As early as 1749, Rev. Mayhew preached a sermon expressing his disagreement with a proposal in the British Parliament, which was intended to impose upon all the American colonies membership in the Episcopal (or Anglican) Church. Such a move would have been disastrous, turning back the clock on much of the American experience. All the hardships the Pilgrims, Puritans, Quakers, Presbyterians, and Huguenots had endured to escape religious persecution in the Old World would have been for naught had England imposed such a requirement on America.

Rev. Mayhew was among the first to see the lethal consequences to Christian freedom that such a parliamentary directive would have had. So, as the British Parliament was discussing the possibility of imposing the Church of England as the State Church in America, Rev. Mayhew preached a message entitled, "Concerning Unlimited Submission to the Higher Powers, to the Council and House of Representatives in Colonial New England." In that message, preached on January 30, 1750, his Scripture passage was Romans 13:1-7; but Rev. Mayhew did not instruct his flock to submit to a tyrant king. He believed there was a time and a place to discuss politics from the pulpit:

> It is hoped that but few will think the subject of it an improper one to be discoursed on in the pulpit, under a notion that this is preaching politics, instead of Christ. However, to remove all prejudices of this sort, I beg it may be remembered that "all Scripture is profitable for doctrine, for reproof, for correction, for instruction in righteousness." Why, then, should not those parts of Scripture which relate to civil government be examined and explained from the desk, as well as others?[22]

> "... it is no easy matter to deceive or conquer a people determined to be free."
>
> Rev. Phillips Payson,
> election sermon, Boston, 1778

Because the Word of God addresses all of life, including politics, Rev. Mayhew concluded that politics is an appropriate topic for the pulpit:

> It is evident that the affairs of civil government may properly fall under a moral and religious consideration. . . . For, although there be a sense, and a very plain and important sense, in which Christ's kingdom is not of this world, his inspired apostles have, nevertheless, laid down some general principles concerning the office of civil rulers, and the duty of subjects, together with the reason and obligation of that duty. . . . [I]t is proper for all who acknowledge the authority of Jesus Christ, and the inspiration of his apostles, to endeavor to understand what is in fact the doctrine which they have delivered concerning this matter.
> . . . .
> Civil tyranny is usually small in its beginning, like "the drop of a bucket," till at length, like a mighty torrent, or the raging waves of the sea, it bears down all before it, and deluges whole countries and empires.[23]

Rev. Mayhew served as another watchman on the wall, warning about this encroachment on liberty. He preached a radical message:

> To say that subjects in general are not proper judges when their governors oppress them, and play the tyrant; and when they defend their rights, administer justice impartially, and promote the public welfare, is as great treason as ever man uttered; – 'tis treason, – not against one single man, but the

state – against the whole body politic; – 'tis treason against mankind; – 'tis treason against common sense; – 'tis treason against God. And this impious principle lays the foundation for justifying all the tyranny and oppression that ever any prince was guilty of.[24]

It was little wonder that the royalist Massachusetts Governor Thomas Hutchinson referred to the clergymen as "seditious." Jonathan Mayhew wasn't alone.

Samuel West

Rev. Samuel West, who graduated from Harvard in 1754 and served as a Congregational minister in Dartmouth, Massachusetts, helped John Adams to write the Constitution of Massachusetts, which although not the first, is the oldest continuing constitution in the world. Rev. West also served on the Massachusetts committee to consider the adoption of the United States Constitution. In an election sermon, West once preached:

> Unlimited submission and obedience is to none but God alone. . . . And to suppose that he has given to any particular set of men a power to require obedience to that which is unreasonable, cruel, and unjust, is robbing the Deity of his justice and goodness.[25]

In July 1776, the same month the Declaration of Independence was signed, Rev. West spoke out in Boston, concerning the Revolution:

> Our cause is so just and good that nothing can prevent our success but only our sins. Could I see a spirit of repentance and reformation prevail throughout the land, I should not have the least apprehension or fear of being brought under the iron rod of slavery, even though all the powers of the globe were combined against us. And though I confess that the irreligion and profaneness which are so common among us gives something of a damp to my spirits, yet I cannot help hoping, and even believing, that Providence has designed this continent for to be the asylum of liberty and true religion.[26]

Rev. John Peter Muhlenberg

In one of the most dramatic moments of the American War for Independence, in a Lutheran church in Virginia, the pastor, Rev. John Peter Muhlenberg, preached from Ecclesiastes 3:1, 8: "To every thing there is a season, and a time to every purpose under the heaven: . . . A time to love, and a time to hate; a time of war, and a time of peace." As Rev. Muhlenberg concluded his sermon, he said: "[I]n the language of Holy Writ, there [is] a time for all things, a time to preach and a time to pray, but those times have passed away . . . there is a time to fight – and that time has now come!"[27]

He then tore off his clergy robe in front of the startled congregation. Under his robe, Rev. Muhlenberg was dressed in the uniform of a Continental Army officer. He declared his intentions to leave the ministry for the duration of the War in order to serve in the cause of American liberty. George Bancroft tells us: "[T]he congregations of Germans, quickened by the preaching of Muhlenberg, were eager to take up arms."[28] This dramatic moment in American history is commemorated by a statue of Muhlenberg that still stands in the U.S. Capitol Rotunda.

> *"Our cause is just."*
>
> Slogan of the Minutemen

William J. Federer tells us what happened next: "That afternoon, at the head of 300 men, he marched off to join General Washington's troops, becoming Colonel of the 8th Virginia Regiment. He served until the end of the war being promoted to the rank of Major-general."[29]

Rev. Muhelnberg's method of recruiting troops was far more dramatic than most, but it is symbolic of the significant role the church and the clergy played in the American Revolution.

The Minutemen

The Minutemen were so named because they could fight at a minute's notice. Often the Minutemen were recruited by their pastor or by the head deacon of their church. It was the pastor or deacon who led them in their military drills. The church was customarily located in the center of town and was usually the hub of society. So when conflict began to brew, it was only natural that the church would continue to be at the center of the activity.

In 1774, the Congress of Massachusetts, recognizing that a significant portion of the colony's military was comprised of Minutemen, commissioned them with this stirring challenge:

> The eyes not only of North America and the whole British Empire, but of all Europe, are upon you. Let us be, therefore, altogether solicitous that no disorderly behavior, nothing unbecoming our characters as Americans, as citizens and Christians, be justly chargeable to us.[30]

Although the Minutemen were poorly equipped volunteers, they used a unique and effective form of warfare for their day. Wars in the late 1700s were customarily fought by lining up armies in columns in the open field and shooting at one another until one or both of the armies retreated. During the Revolutionary War, the British army would line itself up; but the Minutemen, instead of lining up against them in the open field, chose rather to hide behind trees or hills and fight with whatever they could find. Because they had so few guns, the Minutemen were often forced to rely on sticks and rocks to wage their battles against the British army.

The story is told that when the War for Independence was over and America had become a nation, one British general was asked what he had feared most during the war.

"Was it General Washington?"

The general replied, "No, General Washington was a great leader, but I did not fear him the most." Was it the Continental Army, Washington's fighting troops? He replied, "No, they were fine fighters, but I did not fear them the most."

"The weather? The large American cities? The diverse Terrain? The French navy?"

The general replied, "No, I did not fear any of those things the most. The thing that I feared most during the war was the Minutemen. Those crazy soldiers were improperly armed and barely clothed, but the American Minutemen did not know the meaning of the word 'retreat.' If you ever wanted to gain a victory over the Minutemen, you had to kill them all because they never quit."

While this conversation is somewhat modernized, it represents the soul of the Revolution and, hopefully, the soul of those who still stand for freedom to practice a Biblical faith in America.

Lexington and Concord

Perhaps the most famous Minutemen of all were those from the Lexington Church, whose leader was Pastor Jonas Clark of the Black Regiment.

The battles that began on April 19, 1775, in Lexington and Concord sparked the American War for Independence. It was on that date that British soldiers first fired on the Minutemen outside their church in Lexington, Massachusetts. Colonists in what was to become Kentucky were so impressed with the bravery of these Americans in the Bay State that they named one of their own cities Lexington in their honor.

April 19, 1775, was the day the shot was fired that was heard around the world, the shot that ignited the lamp of liberty, a lamp that has since burned around the globe.

Throughout the night of April 18, Paul Revere had made his famous midnight ride, warning, "The British are coming! The British are coming!" The Redcoats were marching to the sleepy little village of Lexington because two of the greatest early patriots of liberty could be found there – Samuel Adams and John Hancock. These two men were being entertained in the home of Rev. Jonas Clark, minister of the church in Lexington.

At that time, Lexington was a small town with a population of about seven hundred. The British were also interested in that area because they were planning to seize a cache of gunpowder being stored in the neighboring town of Concord. George Bancroft tells us what happened in the wee hours of April 19:

> At two in the morning, under the eye of the minister [Rev. Jonas Clark], and of [John] Hancock and [Samuel] Adams, Lexington common was alive with the minute-men; and not with them only, but with the old men, who were exempts, except in case of immediate danger to the town. The roll was called, and, of militia and alarm men, about one hundred and thirty answered to their names. The captain, John Parker, ordered every one to load with powder and ball, but to take care not to be the first to fire[31]

Speaking of the Lexington Church in Massachusetts, Bancroft observed, "How often in that building had they, with renewed professions of their faith, looked up to God as the stay of their fathers and the protector of their privileges!"[32] For a century and a half, Christians had been stepping over that parade ground on their way to church for worship. Now they were there defending their right to continue to worship freely.

Bancroft adds: "The ground on which they trod was the altar of freedom, and they were to furnish the victims."[33] When the two parties – the well-disciplined British Army and the ragtag assembly of church men – encountered each other, it became very clear that the Americans were hopelessly outnumbered, so Captain Parker commanded his men to depart. But before they could do so, the battle began.

In the melee that followed, seven Americans were killed, both the old and the young, and nine were wounded – one sixth of those fighting on the Lexington green. This battle was a turning point for America. Other patriots saw how the Lexington Green was red "with the innocent blood of their brethren slain."[34]

The British, who lost far more men in this first battle, then marched on to Concord. Among the colonial dead left at Lexington were several old men who could easily have gone quietly to their graves in the comfort of their own homes at some future time. Instead, they chose to defend their homes and paid the ultimate price for liberty. This was the sacrificial world of the Minutemen.

Jonas Clark, the minister at Lexington, who lost many of his congregation on the town green that fateful day, said this of the marauding British troops:

> And this is the place where the fatal scene begins! They approach with the morning light; and more like *murderers* and *cutthroats*, than the troops of a *christian king*, without provocation, without warning, when no war was proclaimed, they draw the *sword of violence*, upon the inhabitants of this town, and with a *cruelty* and *barbarity*, which would have made the most hardened savage blush, they *shed* INNOCENT BLOOD. . . . Yonder field can witness the innocent blood of our brethren slain! There the tender father bled, and there the beloved son!

> *"From this day will be dated the liberty of the world."*
>
> Rev. Jonas Clark,
> Commentary on the
> Battle of Lexington,
> April 19, 1776

As Sam Adams examined the field that morning, he proclaimed: "Oh, what a glorious morning is this!"[36] He was not rejoicing in these deaths, but was rejoicing because he knew such a carnage would only hasten the day of complete American independence from Great Britain.

On that same day, the British and Americans exchanged gunfire in nearby Concord. Bancroft notes a spiritual dimension to that battle as well:

> The people of Concord, of whom about two hundred appeared in arms on that day, derived their energy from their sense of the divine power. This looking to God as their sovereign brought the fathers to their pleasant valley; this controlled the loyalty of the sons; and this has made the name of Concord venerable throughout the world.[37]

When word of these battles spread to towns near and far, other Minutemen came pouring in from many places to help their brethren in Lexington and Concord. As an example, George Bancroft notes: "The men of Dedham, even the old men, received their minister's blessing and went forth, in such numbers that scarce one male between sixteen and seventy was left at home."[38] The Dedham minister was another member of the Black Regiment, encouraging his congregation to fight for liberty. The church was clearly the hub of colonial society during our nation's fight for independence.

Give 'em Watts

There were other Minutemen headed by the clergy. During a battle between his parishioners and the British troops, Rev. James Caldwell turned over his church hymnals (full of the hymns of Isaac Watts) when the Minutemen ran out of wadding for their muskets. Running out of wadding was as bad then as running out of bullets would be today. Rev. Caldwell did not hesitate to sacrifice these hymnals, tearing out the pages and handing them to the American soldiers, saying, "Give 'em Watts, boys! Give 'em Watts!" The Minutemen, and Watts, won that battle.

Conclusion

There is much more that could be said about the Black Regiment. Whole books have been written about their influential sermons. Dr. Ellis Sandoz of Louisiana State University has compiled a two-volume set of *Political Sermons of the American Founding Era, 1730-1805*. Dr. Harry Stout, a professor at Yale University, researched Black Regiment sermons that had never been published, and issued his book, *The New England Soul*.

We have seen that the seventh thing every Christian should know about the founding of America is that the Black Regiment, and especially the New England clergy along with their faithful Minutemen, helped to provide the moral and spiritual, as well as the actual, force needed for America to choose liberty and achieve it. As John Wingate Thornton once put it, "To the Pulpit, the Puritan Pulpit, we owe the moral force which won our independence."

Chapter 8
Christian Patriots of Independence

"A good name is rather to be chosen than great riches,
and loving favour rather than silver and gold."
~ Proverbs 22:1

Biblical Christianity was the driving force
behind the key leaders of the American Revolution.

I t has often been said that history is biography. Key people in history
determine events for millions of people, alive and yet unborn. Such was the
case with the key patriots of the Revolutionary era. They were the right
men at the right time, and they each played distinct and significant roles in the
founding of America.

The eighth thing every Christian should know about the founding of
America is that Biblical Christianity was the driving force behind the men who
championed American independence.

George Washington, America's Leader

If America ever had a knight in shining armor riding to her rescue on a
white horse, that knight was George Washington. Ben Hart writes:

> Three major factors caused the American Revolution: a dissident Protestant
> tradition that established a *de facto* independent, self-governing common-
> wealth in New England; heavy-handed, shortsighted, and incredibly inept

British policy; and the emergence of George Washington, a vestryman in Virginia's Anglican Church who brought discipline and decorum to a wild and disorganized band of predominantly radical Protestant-Separatists.[1]

George Washington was truly a great man by everyone's reckoning. His character was remarkable, if we are to believe the judgment of his contemporaries:

- Patrick Henry said: "[I]f you speak of solid information and sound judgment, Washington is unquestionably the greatest man of them all."[2]

- Leading American historian of the 19th century George Bancroft said of Washington: "[H]is qualities were so faultlessly proportioned that the whole people rather claimed him as its choicest representative, the most complete expression of all its attainments and aspirations."[3]

> " . . . *true religion affords to government its surest support.*"
>
> George Washington

- Thomas Jefferson observed: "His integrity was the most pure, his justice the most inflexible I have ever known . . . no motives of interest or consanguinity, of friendship or hatred, being able to bias his decision."[4]

And so Bancroft could conclude:

Wherever he became known, in his family, his neighborhood, his country, his native state, the continent, the camp, civil life, among the common people in foreign courts, throughout the civilized world, and even among the savages, he beyond all other men had the confidence of his kind.[5]

And yet, a few years ago in the new secularist America, a made-for-TV movie about George Washington falsely characterized him as a man who used profane language and was unfaithful to his wife. There is not a shred of historical evidence to support these deceptions. That portrayal told us more about the worldview of the filmmakers than it did about the character of the father of our country. Hollywood had simply taken its own immorality and superimposed it on a larger-than-life historical figure.

Unfortunately, however, since such programs are seen by millions of Americans, and since so many people today are otherwise historically illiterate, many viewers likely believed this fictional slander. Such gross unfairness to a great man who can no longer speak for himself is both tragic and shameful.

If President Washington had been an overly ambitious man, he could have seized ultimate power for himself in America. He could have become a life-long dictator. He was so popular that some men wanted to make him a king, but this idea revolted him. He did not even seek to serve a third term in office. Our nation's first president was of such noble character that he did not want to set a bad precedent for his successors who might want to cling to the reins of power for too long.

General Washington helped to fund the Revolutionary War out of his own pocket. He neither expected nor received any payment for his services. *Compton's Encyclopedia* of 1965 tells us:

He asked no pay beyond his actual expenses, saying that "as no pecuniary consideration could have tempted me to accept this arduous employment at the expense of my domestic ease and happiness, I do not wish to make any profit from it." He rode away at once to Cambridge, Mass., and in July 1775 took command of the Continental Army.[6]

> *"He thought it unwise for one man to hold power so long."*
>
> Compton's Encyclopedia as to why President Washington served only two terms

Washington felt very unworthy of the tasks assigned to him during the War despite his considerable character and talent. He confided to his wife that he did not feel worthy of his position as head of the new nation's army and he needed God's help, writing to her: "I hope my undertaking this service is designed to answer some good purpose. I rely confidently on that Providence which has heretofore preserved and been bountiful to me."[7]

Washington the Deist?

In today's politically correct atmosphere, the very idea that America began as a Christian nation has become controversial. Like so many aspects of our history, we must clear away the popular misunderstandings in order to get at the truth.

There is a great deal of controversy about whether George Washington was truly a Christian or whether he was a Deist. Deists believed in a sort of "clockmaker" god who had wound up the universe, set the world in motion, and then withdrew from any further involvement.

Some of the stories about Washington that are now widely ignored by secularists and others seeking to vilify his character were told fairly soon after his death by Parson Mason Locke Weems. The most famous of these, of course, is the story of little George chopping down the cherry tree and then confessing because he could not tell a lie. Dr. John Eidsmoe, author of *Christianity and the Constitution*, points out that those who want to discredit Washington's character or his thoroughly Christian worldview must first discredit Parson Weems. Writes Eidsmoe: "But for all their attacks, critics have been unable to demonstrate a single clear falsehood in Weems's account."[8]

Even disregarding unsubstantiated stories about our first president as a boy, what we *do* know about Washington for certain is that he had a committed Christian worldview, that he was an active church member, and above all, that He saw the hand of God in the founding of America, including his own role in it. "George Washington the Christian" fits the facts far better than the currently popular notion of "George Washington the Deist."

> "*. . . he used power solely for the public good . . . he was the life and moderator and stay of the most momentous revolution in human affairs . . .*"
>
> George Bancroft

Even the historian Paul Johnson, who believed that Washington probably was a Deist, had to admit that evidence for that proposition is not conclusive. Johnson points out: "Washington himself, who presided at the [constitutional] convention, was probably a deist, though he would have strenuously denied accusations of not being a Christian, if anyone had been foolish enough to make them."[9]

An objective look at some of Washington's own writings and deeds compels one to conclude that either Washington was a genuine Christian, or he was an excellent imposter – a most unlikely scenario.

Evidence of Faith

Washington was without doubt a man of strong faith – faith in God's providence and faith that God was assisting the fledgling new country. We know for certain that Christianity shaped Washington's thinking and worldview, and that his faith gave him immense courage to engage in bold moves that consistently surprised the enemy during the Revolutionary War.

Washington was a committed churchman in a Trinitarian church. At the time of the Revolution, the Anglican Church to which Washington belonged clearly affirmed the authority of the Bible, Jesus' death for sinners, and His bodily resurrection from the dead. Furthermore, Washington was an active church-goer and a servant in the church at a time when only about forty percent of white families in Virginia attended church.[10] Getting to church was not easy in that mostly rural state and often involved a difficult, treacherous ride by horseback along muddy, unpaved roads.

It seems fair to say overall that Washington was a man with a reserved nature. He was not the kind of man who wore his faith on his sleeve, but that does not mean, however, that he was not a man of strong faith.

George Washington had a strong Biblical faith. As a young man it is believed he kept a lengthy prayer journal. Although a copy of this journal was not found until the 1890s – almost a hundred years after his death – some historians believe the journal, called *The Daily Sacrifice*,[11] contained prayers used by General Washington. Here are a few of the entries:

SUNDAY MORNING . . . Almighty God, and most merciful Father, who didst command the children of Israel to offer a daily sacrifice to Thee, that thereby they might glorify and praise Thee for Thy protection both night and day, receive O Lord, my morning sacrifice which I now offer up to Thee.
. . . .
[A]nd since Thou art a God of pure eyes, and will be sanctified in all who draw nearer to Thee, who dost not regard the sacrifice of fools, nor hear sinners who tread in Thy courts, pardon I beseech Thee, my sins, remove them from Thy presence, as far as the east is from the west, and accept me for the merits of Thy son Jesus Christ.
. . . .

> *"I am the Resurrection and the Life; sayeth the Lord. He that believeth in Me, though he were dead yet shall he live. And whosoever liveth and believeth in Me shall never die."*
> *(John 11:25-26)*
>
> Engraving at the tomb of George Washington

Bless my family, kindred, friends and country, be our God and guide this day and forever for His sake, who lay down in the grave and rose again for us, Jesus Christ our Lord. Amen.

SUNDAY EVENING . . . O most Glorious God, in Jesus Christ my merciful and loving Father, I acknowledge and confess my guilt, in the weak and imperfect performance of the duties of this day. I have called on Thee for pardon and forgiveness of sins. . . . Let me live according to those holy rules which Thou hast this day prescribed in Thy holy word.
. . . .
Continue Thy goodness to me this night. These weak petitions, I humbly implore Thee to hear, accept and answer for the sake of Thy Dear Son, Jesus Christ our Lord, Amen.

MONDAY MORNING ... Daily frame [shape] me more and more into the likeness of Thy Son, Jesus Christ, that living in Thy fear, and dying in Thy favor, I may in Thy appointed time attain the resurrection of the just unto eternal life.[12]

These prayers continue daily, all in the same manner of piety. Prayers like these can be found in the Church of England's 1662 *Book of Common Prayer* – which Washington read regularly.

The War Years

When the War for Independence was declared, George Washington was the unanimous choice of the colonies to lead this effort. He proved to be a great military leader, doing much with few resources and little outside backing.

> *"This appointment will have a great effect in cementing the union of these colonies. The general is one of the most important characters of the world; upon him depend the liberties of America."*
>
> John Adams on the appointment of Washington to head the Continental Army

Washington certainly did not relish killing his enemies. His goal was always merely to make it difficult and costly for the British to remain in any one particular spot. Using brilliant strategy, he thrust them out of Boston and later out of Philadelphia. After Washington liberated Boston, Bancroft reports the people there declared their gratitude: "Next to the Divine Power, we ascribe to your wisdom that this acquisition has been made with so little effusion of human blood."[13]

General Washington's first order of the War reflected his serious religious convictions. He commanded that soldiers in the American army should neither curse nor gamble. He reasoned that they would alienate God's superintending care over their just cause if they engaged in such behavior.

Washington ordered that there be no blasphemy, gambling, or abuse of alcohol among the troops. These commands, which were issued on July 4, 1775, are included in Washington's published writings:

> The General most earnestly requires and expects a due observance of those articles of war established for the government of the army, which forbid profane cursing, swearing, and drunkenness. And in like manner he requires and expects of all officers and soldiers, not engaged in actual duty, a punctual

attendance on Divine service, to implore the blessing of Heaven upon the means used for our safety and defense.[14]

There were many times when the hand of God seemed to protect the new nation during the war. For example, in 1776, when Washington and his men were trapped on Brooklyn Heights, Long Island, the British could easily have crushed the American army. In fact, they planned to do just that very thing the next day and bring a quick end to the War.

But Washington engaged in a very bold move. Under cover of fog, he risked evacuating all his troops during the night. He used every ship available, from fishing vessels to rowboats. When morning came, it is reported that the fog remained much longer than normal, just long enough to allow the Americans to cross the Delaware River safely under its protective cover. Events like these prompted Washington to mention often God's providential care in favoring the American cause.

> *"To be prepared for war is one of the most effective means of preserving peace."*
>
> George Washington

During that freezing, terrible winter at Valley Forge, when the Americans were not properly clothed, and many lacked shoes or blankets to protect against the cold, a Quaker (by definition, a pacifist) who lived nearby told his wife upon his arrival at home that he thought the revolutionary side would win the War. Why, his wife asked. Because, said the Quaker, he had been walking in the woods, and had come upon General Washington at prayer. That sight, he said, was enough to shake his view that one could not be a true Christian and a soldier at the same time.

This image of Washington praying in the snow is so commonly depicted that we sometimes take it for granted. But the General's prayer life was legendary. It was reported that he arose early to spend time with God and with the Scriptures and retired early at night to do the same.

Washington once responded to a group of Indians who were seeking to educate their children in the ways of the Englishmen. He told them the single most important thing they could learn from the Americans was the way of Jesus Christ. He said: "You do well to wish to learn our arts and ways of life, and above all, the religion of Jesus Christ. . . . Congress will do everything they can to assist you in this wise intention."[15] This admonition to the Indians flies in the face of today's politically correct secular philosophy and demonstrates that Washington believed:

- Jesus was superior to the Indian gods;
- Western ideals and practices were superior to the ways of Native Americans, and
- Congress would help the Indians learn about the religion of Jesus.

Nothing in this statement supports the current misunderstanding of the First Amendment's "separation of church and state." In fact, the promise of help from Congress to learn the ways of Jesus Christ points in the exact opposite direction.

President Washington believed that God took an active part in the affairs of men. When Benedict Arnold engaged in treason, George Washington stumbled upon the evidence quite by accident; but he believed that God had intervened in making it possible to learn of the treason in time to prevent Arnold from inflicting irreparable damage on the American cause. On that occasion, September 25, 1780, Washington sent the following letter to his troops:

> *"The Divine Author of our Blessed Religion"*
>
> One way in which Washington spoke of Jesus

Happily the treason had been timely discovered to prevent the fatal misfortune. The providential train of circumstances which led to it affords the most convincing proof that the Liberties of America are the object of divine Protection.[16]

President Washington

George Washington was chosen unanimously as President – the only man ever to occupy the office who can make that claim. In his First Inaugural Address, President Washington referred often to God. He exhorted the citizens of the new nation to continue in their reliance on God in order to ensure their liberties because, he said, "the propitious smiles of Heaven can never be expected on a nation that disregards the eternal rules of order and right which Heaven itself has ordained."[17]

Americans today should heed these words of President Washington. So many today want the blessings of God Almighty, but at the same time they clamor for abortion rights, homosexual rights, pornography, promiscuity, and a whole host of things that are contrary to God's revealed will. America cannot have it both ways. We cannot implore a Holy God for His blessings, while insisting at the same time on implementing policies that are clearly contrary to His Word. George Washington knew that to attain God's blessings, the new nation would be obliged to follow God's law.

President Washington chose to be sworn into office with his hand on the Holy Bible, a tradition that continues to this day. At the conclusion of his inauguration as President, Washington bent down and kissed the sacred book. Then he led the Congressmen and everyone else in attendance across the street to St. Paul's Cathedral for a two-hour service of Christian worship to commit the new nation to God. Washington's swearing in occurred in New York City since the Capitol did not move to Washington, D.C. until several years later. The service at St. Paul's had been commissioned by an April 1789 Resolution.[18]

The Congress that resolved to conduct a worship service at St. Paul's following Washington's inauguration was the very same Congress that enacted the First Amendment with its religion clauses. Clearly that first Congress was not concerned about a strict "separation of church and state," as that phrase is misinterpreted and misapplied by courts today.

Washington's Farewell Address, when he left office, has been widely recognized as one of the nation's most important speeches. It contained a warning to the new nation regarding its attention to religion:

> Of all the dispositions and habits which lead to political prosperity, religion and morality are indispensable supports. In vain would that man claim the tribute of patriotism, who should labor to subvert these great pillars of human happiness. . . . And let us with caution indulge the supposition that morality can be maintained without religion.[19]

Washington and Slavery

One modern objection to the thesis that George Washington was a Christian is the fact that he owned slaves. While that is true, it is equally true that he was one of only a few Southerners who took steps to free them upon his death. That is something Thomas Jefferson (who is generally recognized as a Deist) never did. Of our nation's nine slave-owning presidents, Washington was the only one who eventually freed all his slaves.

Meanwhile, the father of our country also worked to end slavery and the slave trade altogether. In the *Fairfax (Virginia) Resolves*, drafted in 1774, George Washington and George Mason solemnly rejected the slave trade, pledging: "After the first day of November next we will neither ourselves import nor purchase any slave or slaves imported by any other person, either from Africa, the West Indies, or any other place."[20] While the *Fairfax Resolves* were a strong denunciation of the slave trade, the British authorities (and most Southern slave holders) were too dependent economically on slavery to support them. These *Resolves* were never enacted.

Samuel Adams

Samuel Adams is often called the lightning rod of the Revolution. He was a dedicated Christian who was hopeful that independence from Britain would mean a return to the God of the original Puritan settlers of New England. Sam Adams was a truly great Christian patriot, yet millions of Americans today are unaware of the critical role he played in the birth of our nation.

> *"Samuel Adams did more than any other American to arouse opposition against English rule in the Colonies."*
>
> Encyclopedia Britannica

Brief Biography

Sam Adams (1722-1803) grew up in a Christian home. His father was a successful businessman, but Sam had no taste for the business and ran it into debt. When he went to Philadelphia to serve in the First and Second Continental Congresses and later to sign the Declaration of Independence, friends had to come and repair his home and barn and give him money for fresh clothing.

Sam's heart was in politics, not business. He studied at Harvard, where his master's thesis was entitled: "Whether it be lawful to resist the Supreme Magistrate, if the Commonwealth cannot otherwise be preserved." He was a cousin of John Adams, who later became the second President of the United States, and he was a particularly gifted writer in advocating for independence. The people of Boston selected him to draft their rejection of the hated Stamp Act in 1764. A year later, he was elected to the colonial assembly of Massachusetts and played a key role in the Boston Town Meetings, where he became an important political force. Adams was also the driving force behind the Boston Tea Party in 1773.

In 1772, Adams created a "Committee of Correspondence" in Boston, in order to keep in touch with his fellow Americans up and down the coast. Similar committees were also formed in the other colonies. David Barton notes that these Committees of Correspondence were created to address a concern similar to one we have today – the people could not trust the mainstream media (royalist newspapers in that day).

Although Sam Adams had signed the Declaration of Independence, he was initially critical of the Constitution. However, when the Bill of Rights was added to guarantee in writing certain liberties – including the right of religious freedom – he championed the cause of the Constitution and, in 1788, successfully led the state of Massachusetts in ratifying it.

The Last Puritan

George Bancroft called Sam Adams "the last of the Puritans."[21] He was a very devout man. His biographer, John C. Miller, says that Samuel Adams cannot be understood without considering the lasting impact Whitefield's preaching at Harvard during the Great Awakening had on him. Some in New England were not touched by the Great Awakening in such a long lasting manner. Miller tells us:

Sam Adams never forgot those stirring days during the Great Awakening when George Whitefield "thundered in the Pulpit against Assemblies & Balls" and New Englanders seemed to turn the clock back to the time of Winthrop and Cotton. The glimpse Adams caught of "Puritanism" in 1740 had profound influence upon his later career. It became one of his strongest desires to restore Puritan manners and morals to New England: in his eyes, the chief purpose of the American Revolution was to separate New England from the "decadent" mother country in order that Puritanism might again flourish as it had in the early seventeenth century. Adams hoped to do by means of a political revolution what George Whitefield had done through a religious awakening. Puritanism was his goal: revolution his method of attaining it.[22]

> *"Neither the wisest constitution nor the wisest laws will secure the liberty and happiness of a people whose manners are universally corrupt."*
>
> Sam Adams

Ideas have consequences. One's theology really does affect one's life. What strengthened Sam Adams, the lighting rod of the American Revolution, was his Biblical faith. This is no minor point. In our day, when our Christian heritage has been all but expunged from the public record, we need to remember that the American most responsible for encouraging the War for Independence was a solid Bible-believing Christian.

He never overlooked an opportunity to give a religious flavor to his political activities. During crises in the struggle between the House of Representatives and the royal governor, Adams set aside days of fasting and prayer to "seek the Lord;" and by this means he gave the American Revolution the character of a moral and religious crusade.[23]

Sam Adams declared (and truly believed) that "providence will erect a mighty empire in America."[24]

"The Rights of Colonists as Christians"

Sam Adams drafted a document in 1772 called "The Rights of the Colonists." It is viewed historically as a key document in articulating the reasons America should sever all political ties to Great Britain. In this document, Adams argued:

> *"[The state] has no right to absolute, arbitrary power over the lives and fortunes of the people; nor can mortals assume a prerogative not only too high for men, but for angels, and therefore reserved for the exercise of the Deity alone."*
>
> Samuel Adams,
> "The Rights of Colonists
> as Subjects," 1772

The right to freedom being the gift of God Almighty . . . the rights of the Colonists as Christians . . . may best be understood by reading and carefully studying the institutions of The Great Law Giver and the Head of the Christian Church, which are to be found clearly written and promulgated in the New Testament.[25]

As writer Robert Flood points out: "Samuel Adams had been telling his countrymen for years that America had to take her stand against tyranny. He regarded individual freedom as 'the law of the Creator' and a Christian right documented in the New Testament."[26] Adams clearly saw the colonists' rights as coming from God and previewed what would several years later become the cornerstone of the Declaration of Independence:

> Among the natural rights of the Colonists are these: first, a right to life; second, to liberty; third, to property; together with the right to support and defend them in the best manner they can. . . [T]he supreme power cannot justly take from any man any part of his property, without his consent in person or by his representative.[27]

Samuel Adams, through the Committees of Correspondence and the Massachusetts Assembly, was one of the first to call for a Continental Congress, a national conference of representatives from the various states. He proposed that the representatives meet in Philadelphia in September 1774, where no army would interrupt their deliberations. He was convinced that "the grievances of America should be radically redressed."[28]

By 1776, two Continental Congress had convened and had accomplished this goal. While the Declaration of Independence was being signed, Sam Adams rejoiced to see that Congress was acknowledging the Lordship of Christ over the affairs of men. He said, "We have this day restored the Sovereign to Whom all men ought to be obedient. He reigns in heaven and from the rising to the setting of the sun, let His kingdom come."[29]

Sam Adams died in poverty, and tragically, in the end, was at least partially disappointed with the outcome of his life's work. The true spiritual revival he had hoped would follow the American Revolution never materialized in his lifetime (although the Second Great Awakening, another frontier American revival, began a few years after his death).

Before his death in 1803, Adams lamented: "I am greatly concerned for my dear native Town [Boston], lest after having stood foremost in the Cause of Religion and Liberty she lose her Glory."[30] Today, in contemplating the decreasing role of Christianity and the Bible in America, it is difficult not to share that concern. This book is intended to alert Christian America that complacency is no longer an option if we are to ensure our continuing liberties.

Patrick Henry

If Samuel Adams was the chief provocateur for independence, Patrick Henry was its greatest orator. Both men received their direction and their strength from their faith in Christ.

Patrick Henry (1736-1799), born in Hanover County, Virginia, was a first cousin once removed to Dolly Madison, wife of Founding Father and fourth President of the United States, James Madison. Henry was well-educated and succeeded as a lawyer at least in part because he was such a gifted speaker. He found his greatest calling in political service and served in the Virginia House of Burgesses, in the first Continental Congress, and later as the first governor of Virginia, an office to which he was repeatedly re-elected. Also in 1776, he helped to write the Virginia constitution.

Like Sam Adams, Henry was initially opposed to the United States Constitution and insisted that a Bill of Rights be added *in writing* before he could support the document. Perhaps because both men were Bible-believing Christians, they understood the true nature of Man – that he is basically sinful and will tend to lord it over his fellow man whenever the opportunity arises, unless checked by a greater power.

Patrick Henry was first and foremost a great orator. He had the "power to rouse man's emotions by the spoken word," says Paul Johnson.[31] He was a firebrand, a rabble-rouser, and an unreflective man of action; but he was also a great statesman, administrator, lawyer and, above all, a serious Christian.

Patrick Henry's most famous phrase was "Give me liberty or give me death," which he delivered on March 23, 1775, before the Virginia Provincial Convention meeting in the House of Burgesses.

The context of this stirring speech was that it was a response to several prior speakers who had argued against preparing for a war with England in defense of their colony. These nay sayers were not necessarily opposed in theory to independence or to fighting the British. Rather, they were concerned, like many other colonists, about a more practical matter – the power and might of the English army compared to the unprepared and disunited ragtag army of the revolutionaries. George Bancroft summarized the attitude of those in the House of Burgesses that day who were against any conflict with England:

> Are we ready for war? . . . Where are our stores, our soldiers, our generals, our money? We are defenseless; yet we talk of war against one of the most formidable nations in the world. It will be time enough to resort to measures of despair when every well-founded hope has vanished.[32]

It was at this point that Patrick Henry rose up among them and, using all his powers of speech, emotion, and intellect, proclaimed:

> For [my] own part [I] consider it as nothing less than a question of freedom or slavery. . . . It is only in this way that we can hope to arrive at truth, and fulfill the great responsibility which we hold to God and our country. . . . Sir, we have done everything that could be done to avert the storm which is now coming on.

> *"Amongst other strange things said of me, I hear it is said by the deists that I am one of their number; and, indeed, that some good people think I am no Christian. This thought gives me much more pain than the appellation of Tory; because I think religion of infinitely higher importance than politics; and I find much cause to reproach myself that I have lived so long and have given no decided and public proofs of my being a Christian. But, indeed, my dear child, this is the character which I prize far above all this world has, or can boast."*
>
> Patrick Henry,
> in a letter to his daughter, 1796

We have petitioned; we have remonstrated; we have supplicated; we have prostrated ourselves before the throne, and have implored its interposition to arrest the tyrannical hands of the ministry and parliament. Our petitions have been slighted; our remonstrances have produced additional violence and insult; our supplications have been disregarded; and we have been spurned, with contempt. . . . We must fight! I repeat it, sir, we must fight! An appeal to arms and to the God of Hosts is all that is left us!

. . . .

Sir, we are not weak, if we make a proper use of the means which the God of nature hath placed in our power. Three millions of people, armed in the Holy cause of liberty, and in such a country as that which we possess, are invincible by any force which our enemy can send against us.

Besides, sir, we shall not fight our battle alone. There is a just God who presides over the destinies of nations, and who will raise up friends to fight our battle for us. The battle, sir, is not to the strong alone; it is to the vigilant, the active, the brave. . . . Is life so dear or peace so sweet as to be purchased at the price of chains and slavery? Forbid it, Almighty God! I know not what course others may take; but as for me, give me liberty or give me death![33]

> *"Bad men cannot make good citizens. It is impossible that a nation of infidels or idolaters should be a nation of freemen."*
>
> Patrick Henry

If Patrick Henry had done nothing in his life but deliver this rousing address to his countrymen in defense of the cause of liberty, he would still be deserving of a place in our nation's history books.

The End of Life

When he was near the end of his life, Patrick Henry said to his family, "Oh, how wretched should I be at this moment, if I had not made my peace with God!"[34] And, as he lay dying, he said to his physician:

Doctor, I wish you to observe how real and beneficial the religion of Christ is to a man about to die. . . . I am, however, much consoled by reflecting that the religion of Christ has, from its first appearance in the world, been attacked in vain by all the wits, philosophers, and wise ones, aided by every power of man, and its triumphs have been complete.[35]

In his Last Will and Testament, Henry again pointed to the teachings of the New Testament as he included this final bequest to his family:

> I have now disposed of all my property to my family; there is one thing more I wish I could give them, and that is the Christian religion. If they had that, and I had not given them one shilling, they would be rich, and if they had not that, and I had given them all the world, they would be poor. This is all the inheritance I give to my dear family. The religion of Christ will give them one which will make them rich indeed.[36]

The language of this bequest has had a recent revival in our own time as some modern American Christians have chosen to include similar words in their own final Will and Testament in order to make one final witness to their faith in Christ.

Conclusion

The greatest orator of the American Revolution, Patrick Henry, was a committed Christian; as was its greatest advocate, Sam Adams; and its greatest leader, George Washington. These men, who together did so much to advance the cause of liberty, were men who first knew liberty of the soul, the liberty Christ brings when He sets a heart free from sin.

So we see that the eighth thing every Christian should know about the founding of America is that Biblical Christianity was the driving force behind the men who championed American independence. America was not founded by Deists; America was founded by Bible-believing Christians. Freedom in Christ led to political freedom, and only freedom in Christ will sustain political freedom. That is a message we urgently need to rediscover in our own day.

Chapter 9
Christianity and the Declaration of Independence

"The law of the Lord is perfect . . . "
~ Psalm 19:7a

Christianity played a significant role in the development of our nation's birth certificate, the Declaration of Independence.

I n America, our rights come from God, not from the state. Therefore, the state cannot take them away. What Uncle Sam gives, Uncle Sam can take away. But our nation's birth certificate, the Declaration of Independence, makes clear that our rights are unalienable because they come from God. Unalienable means that we could not give them away even if we wanted to. Despite the denials of many secular revisionists today, the founders of America declared that our rights and our freedoms come from above, from the God who revealed Himself in the Bible.

The ninth thing every Christian should know about the founding of America is that Christianity played a significant role in the development of our nation's birth certificate, the Declaration of Independence.

The Continental Congress
When the First Continental Congress assembled in Philadelphia in September 1774 to deal with the colonies' worsening relationship with Britain, before getting down to the work at hand the delegates decided to commit the

matter to God. At first, they deliberated about whether to open their sessions with prayer.

John Jay of New York and Edward Rutledge of South Carolina disagreed with the proposal to open in prayer because of the great diversity of denominations present. Samuel Adams then paved the way for the prayer by saying: "I am no bigot. I can hear a prayer from any man of piety and virtue, who is at the same time a friend to his country."[1] Today, he might have said: "I don't care what church a person belongs to, if he's a good Christian and a patriot, I'll join in his prayer."

John Adams recommended for the task, the Rev. Jacob Duché, a local Episcopalian clergyman. The next day, September 7, 1774, was the first day that Congress opened in prayer. That tradition, by the way, has continued ever since. Our present Congress, 230 years later, still opens every session in prayer. The prayer on that first day in 1774, however, was particularly moving. General Washington was present, as were many other Founding Fathers of America – including Patrick Henry, Samuel Adams, his distant cousin John Adams, and John Jay – all joining their hearts together.

> *"Plead my cause, O Lord, with them that strive with me:"*
>
> Opening lines of Psalm 35, read in Congress, September 7, 1774

Jacob Duché did not preach a sermon that morning. Instead he read the entire text of Psalm 35, which was the Episcopal Church's assigned Scripture reading for that day. Here is a portion of what the Founding Fathers heard on that morning of September 7, 1774:

> Plead my cause, O Lord, with them that strive with me: fight against them that fight against me. Take hold of shield and buckler, and stand up for mine help. Draw out also the spear, and stop the way against them that persecute me: say unto my soul, I am thy salvation. Let them be confounded and put to shame that seek after my soul: let them be turned back and brought to confusion that devise my hurt. Let them be as chaff before the wind: and let the angel of the Lord chase them. Let their way be dark and slippery: and let the angel of the Lord persecute them. For without cause have they hid for me their net in a pit, which without cause they have digged for my soul. Let destruction come upon him at unawares; and let his net that he hath hid catch himself: into that very destruction let him fall. And my soul shall be joyful in the Lord: it shall rejoice in his salvation. All my bones shall say, Lord, who is

like unto thee, which deliverest the poor from him that is too strong for him, yea, the poor and the needy from him that spoileth him? . . . Let not them that are mine enemies wrongfully rejoice over me: neither let them wink with the eye that hate me without a cause. For they speak not peace: but they devise deceitful matters against them that are quiet in the land. . . . Let the Lord be magnified, which hath pleasure in the prosperity of his servant. And my tongue shall speak of thy righteousness and of thy praise all the day long (Psalm 35:1-10, 19-20, 27b-28).

There are many Scripture passages that were important in the founding of America, but Psalm 35 was of particular importance to the First Continental Congress.

Later that day, John Adams wrote to Abigail, his wife, encouraging her to look up that Psalm and read it for herself. Here is his first hand account of Rev. Duché's opening prayer at the First Continental Congress, describing the impact Psalm 35 had on these men:

> *"I must beg you to read that Psalm."*
>
> John Adams to Abigail Adams, after Psalm 35 was read in Congress

Accordingly, next morning [Reverend Mr. Duché] appeared with his clerk and in his pontificals, and read several prayers in the established form, and read the collect for the seventh day of September, which was the thirty-fifth Psalm. You must remember, this was the next morning after we heard the horrible rumor of the cannonade of Boston.

I never saw a greater effect upon an audience. It seemed as if heaven had ordained that Psalm to be read on that morning. After this, Mr. Duché, unexpectedly to every body, struck out into an extemporary prayer, which filled the bosom of every man present. I must confess, I never heard a better prayer, or one so well pronounced.

Episcopalian as he is, Dr. Cooper himself [Adams' pastor] never prayed with such fervor, such ardor, such earnestness and pathos, and in language so elegant and sublime, for America, for the Congress, for the province of Massachusetts Bay, and especially the town of Boston. It has had an excellent effect upon everybody here. I must beg you to read that Psalm.[2]

The First Continental Congress adjourned in October 1774 with plans to meet again the following Spring. By the time the Second Continental Congress convened in May 1775, although the colonists had tried every way they could think of to avoid war, the British had made peace impossible. With the battles of Lexington and Concord just a month earlier fresh on their minds, the delegates convened again in Philadelphia.

In 1776, the delegates began the task of drafting their Declaration of Independence from Great Britain. Before declaring their grievances against the king, they first outlined their authority for presenting this official complaint.

Equality Under God

God provided the authority for drafting the Declaration of Independence. The Bible provided the principles that were proclaimed in that document. Christianity taught the world that all men are created equal. But it took a long time, even within Christendom, for this idea to really take hold.

"Voted, That the thanks of Congress be given to Mr. [Jacob] Duché . . . for performing divine Service, and for the excellent prayer, which he composed and delivered on the occasion."

The *Journals of Congress,* September 7, 1774, after Rev. Duché opened Congress in prayer at its request

When America first articulated this Christian ideal in the Declaration of Independence, there were still thousands of men and women on our soil who were not yet being treated as equals because they were slaves. Ultimately, although it has taken more than two hundred years, a bloody Civil War, and an ongoing civil rights movement to achieve it, this doctrine of equality, which has always been enshrined as an ideal in the Declaration, has slowly begun to become a reality for everyone. Today, only the unborn hidden in their mother's wombs remain unequal under the law.

Richard Frothingham, author of *The Rise of the Republic of the United States,* written in 1890, discussed the link between Christianity and the revolutionary idea that all men are created equal:

> [A] low view of man was exerting its full influence when Rome was at the height of its power and glory. Christianity then appeared with its central doctrine, that man was created in the Divine image, was destined for immortality; pronouncing that, in the eye of God, all men are equal. This asserted for the individual an independent value. It occasioned the great inference, that man is superior to the State, which ought to be fashioned for

his use. This was the advent of a new spirit and a new power in the world.[3]

Over two decades ago, in December 1982, on the eve of the International Year of the Bible (1983), *Newsweek* Magazine did a cover story discussing the Bible's impact on America. Many *Newsweek* readers were probably shocked to read these remarkable words:

> [F]or centuries [the Bible] has exerted an unrivaled influence on American culture, politics and social life. Now historians are discovering that the Bible, perhaps even more than the Constitution, is our founding document: the source of the powerful myth of the United States as a special, sacred nation, a people called by God to establish a model society, a beacon to the world.[4]

While Christians might not agree that America's special calling is a "myth," nonetheless, these are incredible words from an unexpected source. A few years later, *Time* Magazine published a similar article called, "Looking to Its Roots," which stated:

> Ours is the only country deliberately founded on a good idea. That good idea combines a commitment to man's inalienable rights with the Calvinist belief in an ultimate moral right and sinful man's obligation to do good. These articles of faith, embodied in the Declaration of Independence and in the Constitution, literally govern our lives today.[5]

> *"Resistance to tyranny becomes the Christian and social duty of each individual . . . Continue steadfast, and with a proper sense of your dependence on God, nobly defend those rights which heaven gave, and no man ought to take from us."*
>
> Resolution by the Massachusetts Provincial Congress, 1774

Even secularists, when they are honest, acknowledge the Christian origins of this nation.

Sources of the Declaration

When Thomas Jefferson wrote the Declaration of Independence, he did so with a great deal of input from those who had gone before him. He did a masterful job of setting forth our nation's reasons for coming into being, but his thoughts were not original. As political science professor, Donald S. Lutz, author of *The Origins of American Constitutionalism*, points out: "[T]here was nothing new in the phrasing and ideas of the Declaration."⁶

Jefferson drew many of his ideas from John Locke and William Blackstone, both Biblical Christians. He also reflected the work of a group of twenty-seven Scotch-Irish Presbyterians in Mecklenburg, North Carolina, who drafted their own Declaration under the direction of Elder Ephraim Brevard, a graduate of Princeton.

The Presbyterians of Mecklenburg declared in May 1775, just as the Second Continental Congress was beginning:

> As all former laws are now suspended in this province, and the congress has not yet provided others, we judge it necessary, for the better preservation of good order, to form certain rules and regulations for the internal government of this country, until laws shall be provided for us by the congress.⁷

Bancroft reports: "The resolves were transmitted with all speed . . . to the British government."⁸ They were then sent by courier to the Continental Congress in Philadelphia. Loraine Boettner adds: "It was the fresh, hearty greeting of the Scotch-Irish to their struggling brethren in the North, and their bold challenge to the power of England." ⁹

Here is what the Presbyterian Elders of North Carolina resolved. We will compare their Mecklenburg Declaration with the nearly identical words (found within the brackets) that Thomas Jefferson later inserted into the Declaration of Independence:

> We do hereby dissolve the political bands which have connected us with the mother-country, ["to dissolve their political bands which have connected them with another"] and hereby absolve ourselves from all allegiance to the British crown ["absolved from all Allegiance to the British Crown"]. . . . Resolved, That we do hereby declare ourselves a free and independent people; are, and of a right ought to be, a sovereign and self-governing Association, under control of no power other than that of our God and the general government of Congress ["by Authority of the good People of these Colonies, solemnly Publish and Declare, That these United Colonies are, and or Right ought to be, Free and Independent States"]; to the maintenance of which we solemnly pledge to each other our mutual cooperation and our lives, our fortunes and our most sacred honor ["we mutually pledge our Lives, our Fortunes, and our sacred Honor"].¹⁰

Jefferson borrows so freely from the work of these Presbyterian elders that today he might be accused of plagiarism. However, in that time, to quote liberally from another source was considered to be a compliment. Author N. S. McFetridge pointed out:

> In correcting his first draft of the Declaration it can be seen, in at least a few places, that Jefferson has erased the original words and inserted those which are first found in the Mecklenburg Declaration. No one can doubt that Jefferson had Brevard's resolutions before him when he was writing his immortal Declaration.[11]

Jefferson's Declaration listed twenty-eight specific violations of the colonists' rights by King George III. Jefferson then concluded: "A Prince, whose Character is thus marked by every act which may define a Tyrant, is unfit to be the Ruler of a free People."[12]

When Jefferson enumerated the king's violations of the rights of the American colonists, he also appears to have drawn from a list of similar abuses articulated in the Constitution of South Carolina, which had been written just a few months earlier. That document also listed twenty-eight specific violations of Great Britain against the American colonists. Political scientist Donald S. Lutz writes: "South Carolina's list contained nineteen of the Declaration's twenty-eight charges."[13] It was apparent that Jefferson had also seen that list in compiling his own.

Historian George Bancroft tells us how Jefferson wrote the Declaration of Independence: "From the fulness of his own mind, without consulting one single book, yet having in memory the example of the Swiss and the manifesto of the United Provinces of the Netherlands, Jefferson drafted the declaration."[14] Thomas Jefferson must have had something akin to a photographic memory. He drew from a large number of sources that were already in existence and tied them together into one magnificent whole.

Most of Jefferson's key sources were English, but there had been one earlier revolution in Europe that provided an important precedent. The Dutch Revolution in the Netherlands had also been influenced by the Reformation. On June 26, 1581, Dutch Calvinists had issued a manifesto declaring their independence from Catholic Spain. The Dutch anchored their declaration of freedom "according to the rights of nature." They declared:

> Every man knows that subjects are not created by God for princes, but princes

for the sake of their subjects. If a prince endeavors to take from his subjects their old liberties, privileges, and customs, he must be considered not as a prince, but as a tyrant; and another prince may of right be chosen in his place as the head.[15]

The spirit of America's Declaration of Independence can be seen in that earlier Dutch declaration.

One of the main themes of America's Declaration was that the king had become tyrannical in his treatment of the colonists. Therefore, he had forfeited his right to rule over them. A group of lesser magistrates (the elected delegates to the Continental Congress) were interposing themselves between the tyrant king and the people, just as the English barons had done at Runnymede in 1215 when they forced King John to grant them certain civil and political liberties through the Magna Carta.

> *"Although the citations came from virtually every part of the Bible, Saint Paul was the favorite in the New Testament, especially the parts of his Epistle to the Romans in which he discusses the basis for and limits on obedience to political authorities."*
>
> Dr. Donald S. Lutz

Biblical Roots of the Declaration

A few decades ago, two political science professors, Donald S. Lutz and Charles S. Hyneman, conducted a ground-breaking, massive study, wherein they examined some 15,000 documents, including several thousand books, written during America's founding era between 1760 and 1805, and analyzed their political content. These men studied political volumes, monographs, pamphlets, and newspaper articles. There they found 3,154 citations or references to other sources.

The source cited or quoted most often in these political writings was the Bible. On average, during that particular half century, 34% of political literary citations came from the Bible.[16] Speaking of that study, David Barton points out, "Four times more often than they quote any individual, they quote the Bible."[17]

After the Bible, the top three sources cited in the political writings of the founding era during the same time period, were Montesquieu, who accounted for 8.3% of the citations; Blackstone with 7.9%; and Locke with 2.9%.[18] All three of these men were professing Christians whose views on politics, government and law were influenced directly and positively by the Bible.

The Enlightenment

Many Americans today have been taught that our revolutionary ideals came from European Enlightenment thinkers. The Enlightenment was an 18th century European philosophical movement that was characterized by rationalism and an impetus toward learning. Many of the Enlightenment thinkers were skeptics with regard to religion and looked to experience for their social and political philosophies; but there were two distinct types of Enlightenment thinkers – those who were skeptics and those who continued to acknowledge God. Early American historian George Bancroft pointed out that it was the Christian Enlightenment thinkers like Montesquieu who influenced our founders, not those like Voltaire who had forsaken God:

> The age could have learnt, from the school of Voltaire, to scoff at its past; but the studious and observing Montesquieu discovered 'the title deeds of humanity,' as they lay buried under the rubbish of privileges, conventional charters, and statutes . . . . He saw . . . that Christianity, which seems to aim only at the happiness of another life, also constitutes man's blessedness in this [one].[19]

> *"The Bible is one of the greatest blessings bestowed by God on the children of men."*
>
> John Locke

Michael Novak also points out that if the Founding Fathers were influenced by the Enlightenment, it clearly was not the atheistic branch of that philosophical movement: "The Founders' Enlightenment was not the Enlightenment of Voltaire; it was the Enlightenment of John Locke, a man ever at pains not to tread heavily on Christian sensibilities."[20]

It was these Christian Enlightenment thinkers, Montesquieu and Locke, along with the legal philosopher, Sir William Blackstone, who most influenced American political thinking during the founding era.

Montesquieu

Baron Charles Louis Joseph de Secondat Montesquieu (1689-1755) was an Enlightenment thinker in one sense, but those who categorize him as a non-believer base their argument on a questionable assumption – essentially guilt by association: "Because he lived in France and taught in French universities during the time of the philisophes, Montesquieu is sometimes identified as a deist."[21] But, according to the 1900 Introduction to his classic work, *The Spirit of the Laws,* author Frederick R. Courdert claims that Montesquieu had been "a devout and consistent Christian."[22]

Whatever the state of his personal salvation, Christianity and the Bible shaped Montesquieu's political worldview. In writing *The Spirit of the Laws*, this philosopher starts with God as the source of all law.

> God is related to the universe, as Creator and Preserver; the laws by which He created all things are those by which He preserves them. He acts according to these rules, because He knows them; He knows them, because He made them; and He made them, because they are in relation to his Wisdom and power.[23]

America's Declaration of Independence was based on the Biblical understanding of the Creator God, as articulated by Montesquieu.

John Locke

> "He that shall collect all the moral rules of the philosophers and compare them with those contained in the New Testament will find them to come short of the morality delivered by our Saviour and taught by His disciples: a college made up of ignorant but inspired fishermen . . . "
>
> John Locke, *A Vindication of the Reasonableness of Christianity*

John Locke (1632-1704) was an English political scientist who had a profound impact on the Founding Fathers of America, including Thomas Jefferson, author of the Declaration of Independence. The classic phrase "life, liberty, and property" is generally attributed to John Locke.

Locke received his master's degree at Christ Church College of Oxford University in 1658 and went on to teach there. Sir James Mackintosh writes: "Educated among the English Dissenters [Puritans and Whigs], during the short period of their political ascendancy, he early imbibed the deep piety and ardent spirit of liberty which actuated that body of men."[24]

Locke became interested in the American colonies, and even wrote the Fundamental Constitutions of the Carolinas in 1663 – the first constitution for what later became two early southern states. His best-known work is *Of Civil Government*, which is a classic in the field of political science and which quotes or cites to the Bible eighty times.

Locke was convinced that humanity's first allegiance must be to God and His Son: "As Men we have God for our King, and are under the Law of Reason: as Christians, we have Jesus the Messiah for our King, and are under the Law reveal'd by him in the Gospel."[25]

Locke also believed that morality was an important component of any society and that morality drew its source from religion, more specifically from the religion of Jesus Christ:

> The study of morality . . . of this there are books enough writ both by ancient and modern philosophers; but the morality of the Gospel doth so exceed them all, that, to give a man a full knowledge of true morality, I shall send him to no other book, but the New Testament.[26]

John Locke was one of Jefferson's main sources for the revolutionary ideas articulated in the Declaration of Independence. And how did Locke's ideas become so well known at the time of our nation's founding? Dr. Lutz answers that question, pointing again to the Black Regiment, those Christian patriots of the pulpit: "It is a little-appreciated irony that the primary avenue for the introduction of Locke's thinking into colonial and revolutionary America was through election-day sermons by the clergy."[27]

Sir William Blackstone

The second most often quoted source in the political writings of the American founding era (outside of the Bible) were the writings of Sir William Blackstone (1723-1780), a British jurist who wrote a popular commentary on British common law. Blackstone believed that Christianity was the basis for British common law. He said: "Christianity was part of the laws of the land."[28] His *Commentaries* have been frequently cited by the United States Supreme Court.[29]

In 1775, Edmund Burke rose up in Parliament to explain why it was that America had such a "fierce spirit of liberty." He pointed out that there was a widespread interest in law in America and that Blackstone's *Commentaries on the Laws of England* were perhaps more popular in the colonies than they were in Britain. Said Burke:

> In no country perhaps in the world is the law so general a study . . . But all who read and most do read endeavor to obtain some smattering in that science. I have been told by an eminent bookseller that in no branch of business, after tracts of popular devotion, were so many books as those on the law exported to the plantations. The colonists have now fallen into the way of printing them for their own use. I hear that they have sold nearly as many Blackstone's Commentaries in America as in England.[30]

One of our earliest United States Supreme Court Justices, Associate Justice James Iredell, said in 1799, in the context of a discussion on the First Amendment:

> We derive our principles of law originally from England . . . in my opinion, no where more happily or just expressed than by the great Author of the Commentaries on the Laws of England, which book deserves more particular regard on this occasion, because for nearly 30 years it has been the manual of almost every student of law in the United States, and its uncommon excellence has also introduced it into the libraries, and often to the favorite reading of private gentlemen.[31]

> " . . . Christianity is part of the laws of the land."
>
> William Blackstone

Blackstone's *Commentaries* were first published in the 1760s; and for the next hundred years, until about the end of the 19th century, quoting or citing to Blackstone typically helped to settle any point on the law. Legal scholar Herbert W. Titus notes:

> At the time of the American Revolution and for over one hundred years afterward, Blackstone's *Commentaries* served as the basic text for lawyers and law students in America. While Blackstone was not a supporter of the American War for Independence, the new nation's lawyers relied upon Blackstone's great treatise as the architectural plan for the building of the America legal system.[32]

God in the Declaration

Our nation's birth certificate, the Declaration of Independence mentions God four times.

- "[T]he Laws of Nature and of Nature's God . . ."
  - referring to God's natural law and to the Holy Scriptures;

- "[A]ll Men are created equal, they are endowed by their Creator with certain unalienable Rights . . ."
  - referring to the Creator God of Genesis;

- "[A]ppealing to the Supreme Judge of the World for the Rectitude of our Intentions . . ."
  - referring to the God revealed in the Holy Scriptures, and

- "[W]ith a firm Reliance on the Protection of Divine Providence . . ."
  – referring to the Biblical God who superintends the affairs of men.[33]

Many critics of Christianity's influence in America like to point out that the Constitution does not mention God or the Bible. However, it was not necessary to mention God in the Constitution because it was the Declaration of Independence that declared for the new nation the foundational principles of freedom, justice, and dependence on God. The Constitution merely added to that founding document the rules by which the new nation would be governed. As the United States Supreme Court said in 1897:

> The first official action of this nation declared the foundation of government in these words: "We hold these truths to be self-evident, that all men are created equal, that they are endowed by their Creator with certain unalienable rights, that among these are life, liberty, and the pursuit of happiness." While such declaration of principles may not have the force of organic law, or be made the basis of judicial decision as to the limits of right and duty, and while in all cases reference must be had to the organic law of the nation for such limits, yet the latter is but the body and the letter of which the former is the thought and the spirit, and it is always safe to read the letter of the constitution in the spirit of the Declaration of Independence.[34]

It could be said that the Declaration of Independence is the "why" of American government, while the Constitution is the "how."

Laws of Nature and of Nature's God

The key to understanding the "spirit of the Declaration" is to understand the phrase, "the laws of Nature and of Nature's God," which is found in the Declaration's introduction:

> When in the Course of human Events, it becomes necessary for one People to dissolve the Political Bands which have connected them with another, and to assume among the Powers of the Earth, the separate and equal Station to which the Laws of Nature and of Nature's God entitle them, a decent Respect to the Opinions of Mankind requires that they should declare the causes which impel them to the Separation.[35]

We think of nature as mountains and trees and animals. We think of nature as describing the qualities of a person or thing. However, in the 18th century the phrase "law of Nature" was understood to be God's general and universal law, written into the creation and understood through reason and science; and the phrase "law of Nature's God" was understood to be God's will as specially revealed to fallen man in the Scriptures.

Blackstone expounds on these two concepts in a section of his *Commentaries* entitled "Of the Nature of Laws in General." Blackstone first explains that God is the source of all law.

> Law, in its most general and comprehensive sense, signifies a rule of action, and is applied indiscriminately to all kinds of action, whether animate or inanimate, rational or irrational. Thus we say, the laws of motion, of gravitation, of optics, or mechanics, as well as the laws of nature and of nations. And it is that rule of action which is prescribed by some superior, and which the inferior is bound to obey.

> Thus, when the Supreme Being formed the universe, and created matter out of nothing, He impressed certain principles upon that matter, from which it can never depart, and without which it would cease to be. When He put that matter into motion, He established certain laws of motion, to which all moveable bodies must conform.[36]

Because God is man's Creator and Superior, God has also imposed certain moral rules of behavior upon him, rules which are as immutable and unchangeable for man and nations as are physical laws like gravity. Blackstone goes on to explain why mankind is obligated to follow the will and law of his Creator:

> Man, considered as a creature, must necessarily be subject to the laws of his Creator, for he is entirely a dependent being. A being, independent of any other, has no rule to pursue but such as he prescribes to himself; but a state of dependence will inevitably oblige the inferior to take the will of him on whom he depends as the rule of his conduct; not, indeed, in every particular, but in all those points wherein his dependence consists . . . [a]nd, consequently as man depends absolutely upon his Maker for everything, it is necessary that he should in all points conform to his Maker's will. *This will of his Maker is called the law of nature.*[37]

We can see in these pious declarations regarding the dependence and subordination of man to God why it has become so important for secularists today to impose on our public school children the theory of Darwinian evolution. Evolution was first suggested in 1859 in Darwin's book, *Origin of the Species*, written nearly a century after Blackstone's *Commentaries* and America's Declaration of Independence. Evolution removes God as the Creator of life and, therefore, releases humanity from any duty to obey His moral laws or to acknowledge His authority in government, as Blackstone and the founders did. The theory of evolution has performed well the role of freeing man from dependence on God; and secularists are reluctant to give it up, even in the face of scientific evidence to the contrary.

Blackstone continues by explaining that man's laws originate with the Creator:

> These are the eternal, immutable laws of good and evil, to which the Creator Himself in all his dispensations conforms; and which He has enabled human reason to discover, so far as they are necessary for the conduct of human actions. Such, among others, are these principles: that we should live honestly, should hurt nobody, and should render to every one his due; to which three general precepts Justinian has reduced the whole doctrine of law.
> . . . .
> This law of nature being . . . dictated by God Himself, is of course superior in obligation to any other. It is binding over all the globe, in all countries, and at all times. No human laws are of any validity if contrary to this; and such of them as are valid derive all their force and all their authority, mediately or immediately, from this original.[38]

Blackstone next explains that man can generally discern the "fixed, uniform and universal" laws of God both in the physical realm and in the realm of human nature through reason:

> [S]o when [God] created man, and endued him with free will to conduct himself in all parts of life, He laid down certain immutable laws of human nature, whereby that free will is in some degree regulated and restrained, and gave him also the faculty of reason to discover the purport of those laws.[39]

But Blackstone quickly moves on to explain the obvious. Because man presently lives in a fallen state, he finds through his own experience "that his reason is corrupt and his understanding full of ignorance and error."[40] Man's reason alone, therefore, is not sufficient to enable him to totally understand

God's natural laws and God's will for men and nations. Therefore, God in his goodness and wisdom also gave man His revealed will written in the Bible. This, according to Blackstone, constitutes "the law of Nature's God."[41] Blackstone explains:

> These precepts, when revealed, are found upon comparison to be really a part of the original law of nature. . . .But we are not from thence to conclude that the knowledge of these truths was attainable by reason, in its present corrupted state; since we find that, until they were revealed, they were hid from the wisdom of ages.[42]

So Blackstone concludes: "Upon these two foundations, the law of nature and the law of revelation, depend all human laws; that is to say, no human laws should be suffered to contradict these."[43] Jefferson has taken Blackstone's phrase, "the law of nature and the law of revelation" and incorporated the concept into the Declaration of Independence as "the laws of Nature and of Nature's God."

Self-Evident Truths

In the Preamble to the Declaration of Independence, Jefferson also spoke of self-evident truths: "We hold these Truths to be self-evident, that all Men are created equal, that they are endowed by their Creator with certain unalienable Rights, that among these are Life, Liberty and the Pursuit of Happiness."[44]

Here Jefferson is referring to truth that is known intuitively as a direct revelation from God without the need for proof, discussion, or debate. For example, there is no need to prove that man is created in the image of God. It is assumed. Black is not white, round is not square, and men are not angels. These are all facts of nature that, as human beings, we are able to reason and understand without further proof.

Jefferson's first self-evident truth is that "all Men are created equal." This equality of all humanity relates to our equality in the sight of God. Before God we all have the same nature – we are all human, we are all sinful, we are all created in His image, and we are all loved by Him. The word "equal" does not mean that we are all in the same circumstances or that we all have the same appearance, ability, assets, character, personality, or status. That truth is also self-evident.

Men are also equal, says Jefferson, in the sense that God created us all with the same self-evident "unalienable rights." Because we are created in God's image, we have a duty to respect and honor the image of God both in ourselves and in others. That duty produces certain corresponding rights. When others try to dishonor the image of God in us, we have both a duty and a right to resist that effort.

These God-given rights, which flow from our duties to God, are sometimes called natural rights – those we possessed under the law of Nature. As part of our birthright, these rights (and duties) can never be sold, given away, or taken from us. Thus, we understand that God, not government, is the source of our rights. Governments are responsible to secure and protect our God-given rights, but governments have no power to grant or deny them. Governments that deny their citizens these rights, Blackstone said, are illegitimate and may be overthrown.

In declaring the endowment of these unalienable rights, Jefferson was clearly influenced by George Mason's "Virginia Declaration of Rights" which said:

> That all men are by nature equally free and independent and have certain inherent rights, of which, when they enter into a state of society, they cannot, by any compact, deprive or divest their posterity; namely, the enjoyment of life and liberty, with the means of acquiring and possessing property, and pursuing and obtaining happiness and safety.[45]

"Those rights then which God and nature have established, and are therefore called natural rights, such as are life and liberty, need not the aid of human laws to be more effectually invested in every man than they are . . . "

William Blackstone

Unalienable Rights

Our Declaration of Independence lists three unalienable rights: "life, liberty and the pursuit of happiness." Our founders believed that these rights were unalienable because citizens possess them whether or not they are recognized by those who govern them. Therefore, it was the duty of the citizen to require that their government secure and protect these rights.

The first two rights are fairly straightforward. The unalienable right to life is a gift from God that could not legitimately be surrendered or taken away.

The unalienable right to life was given to us by God. Our Declaration of Independence requires the state to protect our right to life. Government should not take that right away. When a right is unalienable, even the person who holds that right is not permitted to give it away. Therefore, our government must be accountable for protecting the unalienable right to life for all people regardless of their location, their quality of life, or their burden on the budget. Our Supreme Court breached this unalienable right to life in 1973 when it legalized abortion, the killing of human life in the womb. William Blackstone, in discussing the right to life said: "A man's limbs . . . cannot be wantonly destroyed or disabled without a manifest breach of civil liberty."[46] Is that not precisely what happens in the average abortion, where a child is destroyed by being pulled apart limb by limb?

The second unalienable right granted in our Declaration is the unalienable right to liberty. Blackstone described liberty as consisting "properly in a power of acting as one thinks fit, without any restraint or control, unless by the law of nature."[47] Although unalienable, John Locke tells us: "[T]hough this be a state of liberty, yet it is not a state of licence." Man's liberty may be restrained by the law of Nature which teaches that:

> *"If American democracy is to remain the greatest hope of humanity, it must continue abundantly in the faith of the Bible."*
>
> Calvin Coolidge

[B]eing all equal and independent, no one ought to harm another in his life, health, liberty or possessions; for men being all the workmanship of one omnipotent and infinitely wise Maker; all the servants of one sovereign Master, sent into the world by His order and about His business; they are His property, whose workmanship they are made to last during His, not one another's pleasure.[48]

The last unalienable right in the Declaration is "the Pursuit of Happiness." There is an intentional direct link, says Blackstone, between our happiness and God's law:

> [God] has not perplexed the law of nature with a multitude of abstracted rules and precepts, referring merely to the fitness or unfitness of things, as some have vainly surmised; but has graciously reduced the rule of obedience to this one paternal precept, "that man should pursue his own happiness." This is the foundation of what we call ethics, or natural law.[49]

Like Locke, Blackstone does not equate the pursuit of happiness with license, as so many in America do today. Instead, he explains that a man's true happiness can only be found in obedience to God's law: "For He has so intimately connected, so inseparably interwoven the laws of eternal justice with the happiness of each individual, that the latter cannot be attained but by observing the former."[50] The "pursuit of happiness" is not a hedonistic concept.

Our Declaration of Independence clearly says that the government's purpose is to "secure" these unalienable rights of the people, not to grant or deny them.

Final Words

In Jefferson's climactic closing to the Declaration of Independence, he appealed "to the Supreme Judge of the World for the rectitude of our intentions." Only God could validate the moral correctness of their movement for independence from Great Britain. Only God could grant them success in their historic endeavor. This small band of patriots was challenging the most powerful nation in the world at that time. Jefferson reinforced this appeal by ending the Declaration with these words: "And for the support of this Declaration, with a firm Reliance on the Protection of divine Providence, we mutually pledge to each other our Lives, our Fortunes, and our sacred Honor."[51]

In 1776, people were very familiar with the term "divine Providence." It meant God's care for His people and His superintending control of the world. It was divine Providence that would be required to see them safely through the War. It was their faith in God and their confidence that independence was morally right and was God's will for America that gave these delegates the courage to pledge their lives, their fortunes, and their sacred honor to this cause. They knew that if they were unsuccessful they would indeed have much to lose.

Conclusion

John Adams proposed that when America's future citizens celebrated the Declaration of Independence, they should have religious services to thank God for what He had brought about. President Adams said Independence Day should "be celebrated by succeeding generations as the great anniversary festival, commemorated as the day of deliverance, by solemn acts of devotion to God Almighty, from one end of the continent to the other, from this time forward and forevermore."[52]

The ninth thing every Christian should know about the founding of America is that Christianity played a significant role in the development of our nation's birth certificate, the Declaration of Independence. And so Paul Johnson can write:

There is no question that the Declaration of Independence was, to those who signed it, a religious as well as a secular act, and that the Revolutionary War had the approbation of divine providence. They had won it with God's blessing and, afterwards, they drew up their framework of government with God's blessing, just as in the 17th century the colonists had drawn up their Compacts and Charters and Orders and Instruments, with God peering over their shoulders.[53]

Chapter 10
Christianity and the Constitution

"Except the Lord build the house, they labour in vain that build it: . . ."
~ Psalm 127:1a

The Biblical understanding of the sinfulness of man was the guiding principle behind the United States Constitution.

E ven as our Founding Fathers were agonizing and compromising over the details of the Constitution, many of them recognized that something great was taking place among them. They were pursuing a course that had never before been pursued in all of human history. They were creating a document that would provide the newly independent colonies with self-government and freedom. Since then, the model they crafted has been admired and copied around the world. But before America gave the gift of self-government to the world, God gave the gift of freedom and self-government to America.

The tenth thing every Christian should know about the founding of America is that the Biblical understanding of the sinfulness of man was the guiding principle behind the United States Constitution. The framers of the Constitution drew their inspiration from the Bible. They intended for America to be one nation under God. They had no intention of establishing an agnostic or atheistic state.

Revolution Not a Bloodbath

The American Revolution was very different from other revolutions around the globe, which have generally ended with bloodbaths and failure. America had a revolution. But it was a revolution under God, not a secular revolution like the French Revolution in 1789, which ended with the guillotine, or the Bolshevik Revolution of 1917, which ended with the gulags.

The founders of America saw God as a major part of the whole revolutionary process. They conducted their revolution and organized their new nation under the laws of God. On the other hand, as Michael Novak pointed out: "The dogmatic atheism of the continental Enlightenment and of German historicism left their proponents stranded on the shoals of tyrannical fanaticism – from Robespierre to Pol Pot."[1] Because our founders believed in the Biblical concept of man's sinfulness, they gave us a much more secure form of government than the post-revolutionary governments, such as that of Robespierre and the Jacobins in France, which were based on the assumption that men (or at least some men like the "workers" or the "proletariat") are basically good.

Since the American and French Revolutions occurred within a decade of each other, the contrast between these two is especially pertinent. The most striking difference between our Founding Fathers and the French revolutionaries was that the founders of America began with the assumption that man is basically evil; therefore, citizens must protect themselves even from those who run the government. The founders were well-acquainted with verses like Jeremiah 17:9, which declares: "The heart is deceitful above all things, and desperately wicked: who can know it?"

In contrast, the French Revolution began with the teachings of Jean Jacques Rousseau and other secular Enlightenment thinkers, who believed that man was basically good and, therefore, the people could remake government in their own image. But Rousseau's idealistic, utopian, unrealistic, and unbiblical view of man led to a relentless bloodbath both during and after the French Revolution. The revolution that was based on the basic goodness of man was destroyed by man's sinfulness. France has gone through a dozen overhauls of its governmental system in the last two hundred years, with several new constitutions being required, while during the same time period, the United States has been ruled by only one Constitution.[2]

The Federalist Papers

After the Constitution was drafted in 1787, it had to be ratified by nine of the thirteen colonies before it could become the law of the land. Because New York was such a pivotal swing state in the approval process for the new Constitution, a series of anonymous pro-Constitution letters began to appear in the newspapers there under the pseudonym "Publius." These eighty-five letters to the editor came to be known as *The Federalist* (sometimes called *The Federalist Papers*). They help to shed light on what the founders intended by the Constitution, since they were written contemporaneously by those who had helped to frame that document.

The Federalist Papers should be required reading for all American law students, as should the Declaration of Independence and the Constitution. Most Americans are shocked to discover that these foundational documents are not required reading in most law schools. Therefore, many law students graduate, pass the bar exam, and begin to practice law without having even a vague understanding of the overarching Biblical principles that formed our nation, its Constitution, and its laws.

The real identity of "Publius" was not known in 1789, but we know today that *The Federalist Papers* were written by Alexander Hamilton, James Madison, and John Jay. All three of these writers professed faith in Jesus Christ. Their essays are still sometimes cited in legal briefs and quoted in various court decisions.

Father of the Constitution

James Madison, one of the authors known as "Publius," played an especially significant role in shaping the American Constitution. Some have called him the father of the Constitution or its chief architect. Others claim this title is an exaggeration. Historian Donald S. Lutz pointed out: "Madison's own notes are the proof that he was not the primary framer of the Constitution, but was part of a process that prominently involved many others."[3] Whichever view one adopts, there is no question that Madison's influence in helping to frame the new government was invaluable. And Madison's view of government and law was primarily shaped by his Biblical Christianity.

As a Virginian, one would have expected James Madison to study at the Anglican college of William and Mary. Instead, he chose to attend a Calvinist school, the College of New Jersey (now called Princeton) where he sat under the direct tutelage of Dr. John Witherspoon, the prominent Presbyterian patriot who was the only minister to sign the Declaration of Independence. Bishop Meade said this of Madison:

Mr. Madison was sent to Princeton College – perhaps through fear of the skeptical principles then so prevalent at William and Mary. During his stay at Princeton a great revival took place, and it was believed that he partook of its spirit. On his return home he conducted worship in his father's house. He soon after offered for the Legislature, and it was objected to him, by his opponents, that he was better suited to the pulpit than to the legislative hall.[4]

Madison learned his lessons well under Dr. Witherspoon. In 1785, in his classic essay, *Memorial and Remonstrance*, Madison seems to echo Roger Williams of Rhode Island:

> *"All men having power ought to be distrusted."*
>
> James Madison

Whilst we assert for ourselves a freedom to embrace, to profess, and to observe the religion which we believe to be of divine origin, we cannot deny an equal freedom to those whose minds have not yet yielded to the evidence which has convinced us. If this freedom be abused, it is an offence against God, not against man: To God therefore, not to men, must an account of it be rendered.[5]

Since God will be the ultimate judge of all human consciences, it is the obligation of government to grant all citizens the freedom to believe as their consciences dictate. These ideas would come to the forefront again when Madison helped draft the First Amendment to the Constitution, part of a written Bill of Rights which many Americans required before they would sign or endorse the new Constitution.

Perhaps the most important lesson Madison learned from his Princeton education was his firm belief in the Biblical doctrine of man's inherent sinfulness. Because of man's sin, government must institute a rigorous system of checks and balances to protect its citizens from tyranny. Eidsmoe writes:

> "[A]lthough Witherspoon derived the concept of separation of powers from other sources, such as Montesquieu, checks and balances seem to have been his own unique contribution to the foundation of U. S. Government."[6]

Rev. Witherspoon's strong Calvinist theology greatly influenced Madison's philosophy of political science. Madison wrote in *Federalist #10*: "It is in vain to say that enlightened statesmen will be able to adjust these clashing interests and render them all subservient to the public good. Enlightened statesmen will not always be at the helm."[7]

Then, in *Federalist #47*, Madison explained why governmental power had to be divided between competing forces: "The accumulation of all powers, legislative, executive, and judiciary, in the same hands, whether of one, a few, or many, and whether hereditary, self-appointed, or elective, may justly be pronounced the very definition of tyranny."[8] Having so recently escaped from one tyrant in England, the drafters of the Constitution were careful not to merely replace him with another.

And so Eidsmoe concludes: "One thing is certain: the Christian religion, particularly Rev. Witherspoon's Calvinism, which emphasized the fallen nature of man, influenced Madison's view of law and government."[9] His concept of checks and balances took into account the temptation in man's nature to greed and selfishness. It withdrew from any one man, or from any group of men, the power to become tyrannical.

> *"Religion is the only solid basis of good morals; therefore education should teach the precepts of religion, and the duties of man toward God . . ."*
>
> Gouverneur Morris,
> Constitution signer

Belief in Man's Sinfulness

James Madison was not alone among the founders in professing the Christian doctrine of original sin and insisting that this theological concept be incorporated into the new government through an elaborate system of checks and balances. The Founding Fathers all knew that because man was sinful, power could not be vested in any one person. Echoing Scripture, even though he generally claimed not to believe it, Benjamin Franklin declared: "There is scarce a king in a hundred who would not, if he could, follow the example of Pharaoh, get first all the peoples' money, then all their lands and then make them and their children servants forever."[10]

Similarly, John Adams, of Puritan New England, saw any man who held political power as "a ravenous beast of prey." That power, he believed, must be contained and balanced by other governmental powers.[11]

Alexander Hamilton

Alexander Hamilton, another of the trio of men who wrote in New York as "Publius," was a practicing Episcopalian with a Dutch Reformed background who routinely led his family in prayers.[12] Two years before he died, he proposed the formation of a Christian society that would spread both Christianity and the principles of the Constitution. He wrote to a friend, James Bayard:

> In my opinion, the present constitution is the standard to which we are to cling. Under its banner bona fide must we combat our political foes, rejecting all changes but through the channel itself provided for amendments. By these general views of the subject have my reflections been guided. I now offer you the outline of the plan they have suggested. Let an association be formed to be denominated "The Christian Constitutional Society," its object to be first: The support of the Christian religion. Second: The support of the United States.[13]

> *"Till the millennium comes, in spite of all our boasted light and purification, hypocrisy and treachery will continue to be the most successful commodities in the political market."*
>
> Alexander Hamilton

Hamilton's premature death in 1804 in a duel in which he was reluctant to participate and in which he chose not to shoot at his opponent, Aaron Burr, ended any plans for establishing "The Christian Constitutional Society." Perhaps God will one day raise up someone, perhaps even a reader of this book, to establish what Hamilton only dreamed of.

Hamilton recognized what the French revolutionaries never understood – that humanity has not yet been perfected. Arguing for the adoption of the Constitution with its separation of powers and its clear understanding of the limits of government, he wrote in *Federalist #6*:

> Is it not time to awake from the deceitful dream of a golden age and to adopt as a practical maxim for the direction of our political conduct that we, as well as the other inhabitants of the globe, are yet remote from the happy empire of perfect wisdom and perfect virtue?[14]

Hamilton added in *Federalist #15*, "Why has government been instituted at all? Because the passions of men will not conform to the dictates of reason and justice without constraint."[15]

"Publius" also emphasized that there were some positive traits citizens would need to possess in order for the new government to be successful. *Federalist #55*, which is generally attributed to either Hamilton or Madison, discusses the necessity, in a republican (or representative) form of government, for both the electors and those elected to be of good character:

As there is a degree of depravity in mankind which requires a certain degree of circumspection and distrust, so there are other qualities in human nature which justify a certain portion of esteem and confidence. Republican government presupposes the existence of these qualities in a higher degree than any other form. Were the pictures which have been drawn by the political jealousy of some among us faithful likenesses of the human character, the inference would be that there is not sufficient virtue among men for self-government; and that nothing less than the chains of despotism can restrain them from destroying and devouring one another.[16]

Power to the People

Following the example of the self-governing compacts, covenants and constitutions previously drafted in Puritan New England and in the other colonies, the men who drafted our Constitution also believed that the best government rests in the authority of the people. Alexander Hamilton pointed out in *Federalist #22*, "The fabric of the American empire ought to rest on the solid basis of THE CONSENT OF THE PEOPLE. The streams of national power ought to flow immediately from that pure, original fountain of all legitimate authority."[17]

> *"That honourable determination which animates every votary of freedom, to rest all our political experiments on the capacity of mankind for self-government."*
>
> James Madison,
> *Federalist #39*

Madison echoed the same thought in *Federalist #49*: "[T]he people are the only legitimate fountain of power, and it is from them that the constitutional charter, under which the several branches of government hold their power, is derived."[18]

By placing the authority of government in the consent of the governed, our founders recognized that ultimately, through the legislature, the majority – "we the people" – were to have the greater say. Madison points out: "[I]n republican government the majority however composed, ultimately give the law."[19] Today, in America, we have seen that when secularists do not have a sufficient majority to enact legislation favorable to them, they have taken an alternate route to establish their anti-God agenda through sympathetic judges.

To clarify what our founders meant when they established a republic and not a democracy, Madison, in *Federalist #14*, pointed out the difference: "It is that in a democracy the people meet and exercise the government in person; in a republic they assemble and administer it by their representatives and agents. A democracy, consequently, must be confined to a small spot. A republic may be extended over a large region."[20]

John Adams once said, in arguing for the superiority of a republic over a democracy: "There is no good government, but what is republican; for a republic is an empire of laws, and not of men; and, to constitute the best of republics, we enforced the necessity of separating the executive, legislative, and judicial powers."[21]

Most of the founders were quite leery of the whole concept of a pure democracy, where the people hold all power directly. Instead, the founders established this nation as a republic, in which the government functions through elected officials. In *Federalist #10*, Madison reveals one of the most serious problems that can arise in a true democracy:

> *"A republic, by which I mean a government in which the scheme of representation takes place . . . "*
>
> James Madison,
> *Federalist #10*

[A] pure democracy, by which I mean a society consisting of a small number of citizens, who assemble and administer the government in person, can admit of no cure for the mischiefs of faction. A common passion or interest will, in almost every case, be felt by a majority of the whole.[22]

Additionally, in the same *Federalist*, Madison argued that a republic is to be preferred over a democracy because, through elected officials, the government can more effectively deal with deep-seated disagreement of opinions. He speaks of the "advantage which a republic has over a democracy in controlling the effects of faction."[23] One of the problems we see today in modern America, where the judiciary has assumed a greater power than the legislature, is that factionalism has been magnified through court appointments that lead to the political ascendancy of one unelected faction or another.

The men who drafted the Constitution viewed the legislative branch as being far more important than the judicial branch. In fact, as the original founders interpreted the Constitution, the judiciary was expected to be the least important branch of government. Article I of the Constitution (dealing the with the legislature) received much more detailed attention than Article III (dealing with the judiciary). The Founding Fathers never intended for us to live under a "Judge-ocracy," where the federal Supreme Court would rule as an oligarchy and impose the will of the minority on the majority.

Hamilton points out in a footnote in *Federalist #78*: "The celebrated

Montesquieu, speaking of them [the three branches of government], says: 'Of the three powers above mentioned, the JUDICIARY is next to nothing.'"[24] In the same *Federalist*, Hamilton discusses the constitutional purpose of the judiciary:

> It is far more rational to suppose that the courts were designed to be an inter-
> mediate body between the people and the legislature in order, among other
> things, to keep the latter within the limits assigned to their authority. The
> interpretation of the laws is the proper and peculiar province of the courts.[25]

A Virtuous People

Our founders understood that a Constitutional government that placed ultimate power in the hands of the people would ultimately require a virtuous people in order to succeed. Therefore, the Black Regiment was expected to assume an important role.

> "The interpretation of the laws is the proper and peculiar province of the courts."
>
> Alexander Hamilton,
> *Federalist #78*

Seven years before the United States Constitution was written, Massachusetts unveiled its state constitution. One of the influential members of the Black Regiment, Rev. Samuel Cooper of Boston, delivered a sermon in honor of that occasion entitled "A Sermon on the Day of the Commencement of the Constitution." Rev. Cooper discussed the importance of virtue in maintaining good government:

> Virtue is the spirit of a republic; for where all power is derived from the
> people, all depends on their good disposition. If they are impious, factious and
> selfish; if they are abandoned to idleness, dissipation, luxury, and extravagance;
> if they are lost to the fear of God, and the love of their country, all is lost.[26]

In this sermon, Rev. Cooper predicted a great future for America if she pursued a Godly course:

> Rome rose to empire because she early thought herself destined for it. . . . We
> have before us an object more truly great and honourable. We seem called by
> heaven to make a large portion of this globe a seat of knowledge and liberty,
> of agriculture, commerce, and arts, and what is more important than all, of
> Christian piety and virtue.[27]

American Christians need to understand what is at stake today in our nation. Since the 1960s, because of various decisions by the United States Supreme Court favoring secularism over religion, America has begun to stray from its founding Biblical principles. America seems to have forgotten God. We regularly break His laws and no longer think them important to our survival as a nation. Courts have jettisoned major portions of our Judeo-Christian heritage as unconstitutional. We must not forget what John Adams, our second President and signer of the Declaration of Independence, said about virtue being an implied assumption of our constitutional form of government. He warned his countrymen:

> [W]e have no government armed with power capable of contending with human passions unbridled by morality and religion. Avarice, ambition, revenge, or gallantry, would break the strongest cords of our Constitution as a whale goes through a net. Our Constitution was made only for a moral and religious people. It is wholly inadequate to the government of any other.[28]

> *"And the most fundamental assumption [of the Constitution] is that the American people are a virtuous people."*
>
> Donald S. Lutz,
> *The Origins of American Constitutionalism*

The Proceedings

The vast majority of delegates who attended the Constitutional Convention were professing Christians. Only Benjamin Franklin and James Wilson of Pennsylvania were known to be Deists, while Hugh Williamson of North Carolina and James McClurg of Virginia may also have been non-Trinitarian. John Eidsmoe, author of *Christianity and the Constitution*, concludes that, at most, 5.5% of those attending the Constitutional Convention were Deists.[29]

When the colonial representatives first met in 1787 for what we now call the Constitutional Convention, they were not meeting for the purpose of drafting a brand new constitution. Instead, they merely wanted to revise their contemporary framework of government, the Articles of Confederation, written in 1777 and ratified in 1781. That government, which was based on a loose confederation of the states, had been operating since the end of the War for Independence in 1783, but it no longer seemed sufficient for the needs of the uniting states. Alexander Hamilton said of the nation under the Articles of Confederation in *Federalist #30*: "In America . . . the government of the Union has gradually dwindled into a state of decay, approaching nearly to annihilation."[30]

Soon after the delegates first began their attempt to revise the Articles of Confederation, Edmond Jennings Randolph, representing Virginia, stood up and proposed a complete overhaul of the Articles although, ironically, by the end of the Convention, he chose not to sign the document because he disagreed with the direction it had taken.

Like virtually every early American document, the Articles of Confederation mentioned God, referring to Him as "the Great Governor of the World."[31] But there were structural flaws in the Articles, making that document unworkable. One such flaw was that every legislative measure had to be approved by *all* of the states, and getting all the states to agree on anything was very difficult.

To make a more workable government, the Constitutional Convention decided to include the provision that it would take only nine of the thirteen states, essentially a two-thirds majority, for proposals to pass. This would also be the same majority required for ratification of the new document. Nevertheless, even with only nine states required for agreement, the changes did not come easily.

> *"And whereas it has pleased the Great Governor of the World to incline the hearts of the Legislatures we respectively represent in Congress, to approve of, and to authorize us to ratify the said Articles of Confederation and perpetual union."*
>
> Articles of Confederation, 1778, forerunner to the Constitution

The Miracle at Philadelphia

We tend to glamorize the writing of the Constitution, however, the process was anything but glamorous. The Convention met at Independence Hall in Philadelphia between May and September of 1787. The weather was hot and muggy. The pace was slow going. Tempers flared. The delegates seemed to go around and around in circles for weeks on end. Some delegates left – prematurely and permanently.

There was a great deal of acrimony at the Convention, especially between the more populated states and the less populated states as they discussed how they should be represented in the new united government. There were also bitter conflicts over slavery as some, particularly in the North, loathed the practice, while others, particularly in the South, depended upon it for their economic viability.

In light of all the difficulties encountered in writing the Constitution, Alexander Hamilton could reflect back years later about the Constitutional government that had emerged from this Convention: "For my own part,

I sincerely esteem it a system which without the finger of God, never could have been suggested and agreed upon by such a diversity of interests."[32]

The Convention proceedings were so difficult that at one point, when Alexander Hamilton had left temporarily, George Washington wrote him a letter, complaining about the whole business: "I *almost* despair of seeing a favourable issue to the proceedings of the Convention, and do therefore repent [of] having had any agency in the business."[33] The convention was deteriorating so badly that even Washington, its president, was beginning to regret being there.

When the delegates had finally agreed on a workable Constitution and the Convention had adjourned, Washington saw the outcome as miraculous:

> *Ben Franklin's opinion of the Constitutional Convention: "He says it is the most august and respectable assembly he ever was in in his life."*
>
> Catherine Drinker Bowen

It appears to me, then, little short of a miracle, that the Delegates from so many different States (which States you know are different from each other) in their manners, circumstances, and prejudices), should unite in forming a system of national Government, so little liable to well founded objections.[34]

In *Federalist #37*, James Madison clearly articulated his belief that a supernatural work of God had taken place in Independence Hall:

The real wonder is that so many difficulties should have been surmounted, and surmounted with a unanimity almost as unprecedented as it must have been unexpected. It is impossible for any man of candor to reflect on this circumstance without partaking of the astonishment. It is impossible for the man of pious reflection not to perceive in it a finger of that Almighty hand which has been so frequently and signally extended to our relief in the critical stages of the revolution.[35]

Author Catherine Drinker Bowen described the atmosphere at the Convention on June 9, 1787. The proceedings, which had begun in May, seemed to be going nowhere: "At this point and indeed throughout the month of June, one marvels the Convention did not dissolve and the members go home. The large states were if possible more stubborn than the small."[36]

By June 28, 1787, things had not improved. Writes Bowen: "A Georgia delegate, William Few, described that morning of June twenty-eight as 'an awful and critical moment. If the Convention had then adjourned, the dissolution of the union of the states seemed inevitable.'"[37]

But something happened.

There was a breakthrough.

Ben Franklin's Speech

The great turning point in the Convention came on June 28, after weeks and weeks of frustratingly little progress. It was at that time that Benjamin Franklin, a man who never claimed to be born again, made an impassioned speech, reminding his fellow delegates that God had always answered their prayers as a nation, even when they were at war. Now that things were going so badly, should they not again turn to the Lord for help? Besides, asked Franklin, how could they expect to create a new nation successfully without God's help? Here are Dr. Ben Franklin's own words on that miraculous day:

> Mr. President: The small progress we have made after four or five weeks close attendance & continual reasonings with each other – our different sentiments on almost every question, several of the last producing as many noes as ayes, is methinks a melancholy proof of the imperfection of the Human Understanding.
>
> We indeed seem to feel our own want of political wisdom, since we have been running about in search of it. We have gone back to ancient history for models of government, and examined the different forms of those Republics which, having been formed with the seeds of their own dissolution, now no longer exist. And we have viewed Modern States all round Europe, but find none of their Constitutions suitable to our circumstances.
>
> In this situation of this Assembly, groping as it were in the dark to find political truth, and scarce able to distinguish it when presented to us, how has it happened, Sir, that we have not hitherto once thought of humbly applying to the Father of lights to illuminate our understanding?
>
> In the beginning of the Contest with G. Britain, when we were sensible of danger, we had daily prayer in this room for Divine protection – Our prayers, Sir, were heard, & they were graciously answered. All of us who were engaged in the struggle must have observed frequent instances of a superintending Providence in our favor.

The Constitutional Convention was often slow-going and discouraging. "George Mason had said he would bury his bones in Philadelphia rather than quit with no solution found."

Catherine Drinker Bowen

To that kind Providence we owe this happy opportunity of consulting in peace on the means of establishing our future national felicity. And have we now forgotten that powerful Friend? or do we imagine we no longer need His assistance?

I have lived, Sir, a long time, and the longer I live, the more convincing proofs I see of this truth – that God Governs in the affairs of men. And if a sparrow cannot fall to the ground without His notice, is it probable that an empire can rise without His aid?

We have been assured, Sir, in the Sacred Writings, that "except the Lord build the House, they labor in vain that build it." [Psalm 127:1a] I firmly believe this; and I also believe that without his concurring aid we shall succeed in this political building no better than the Builders of Babel: We shall be divided by our partial local interests; our projects will be confounded, and we ourselves shall become a reproach and bye word down to future ages.

> "An atmosphere of reconciliation appeared to descend over the convention hall."
>
> Benjamin Hart,
> *Faith and Freedom,*
> commenting on the mood following Ben Franklin's plea for prayer

And what is worse, mankind may hereafter from this unfortunate instance, despair of establishing Governments by Human wisdom and leave it to chance, war and conquest.

I therefore beg leave to move – that henceforth prayers imploring the assistance of Heaven, and its blessing on our deliberations, be held in this Assembly every morning before we proceed to business, and that one or more of the clergy of this city be requested to officiate in that service.[38]

Here was probably the least religious of the Founding Fathers calling for prayer and quoting Scripture. Here was the honorable statesman, Dr. Franklin, making an impassioned and Biblical speech at a critical moment.

Immediately after Franklin spoke, Roger Sherman of Connecticut seconded his motion for prayer. Many of those who saw and heard the oldest man among them make this earnest plea were deeply moved. New Jersey delegate Jonathan Dayton reported what he saw after Dr. Franklin's impassioned request for prayer:

The Doctor sat down; and never did I behold a countenance at once so dignified and delighted as was that of Washington at the close of the address;

nor were the members of the convention generally less affected. The words of the venerable Franklin fell upon our ears with a weight and authority, even greater that we may suppose an oracle to have had in a Roman senate![39]

But there were others who had their own practical reasons for being opposed to the motion to begin each day with prayer. John Eidsmoe reports:

The motion for opening the sessions with prayer every morning was not acted on because the Convention lacked funds to pay a clergyman, and because the delegates were afraid that news of outside clergymen coming to assist in services would start rumors that dissension was breaking out in the Convention.[40]

Edmund Jennings Randolph of Virginia proposed a compromise measure: "That a sermon be preached at the request of the convention on the 4th of July, the anniversary of Independence; & thenceforward prayers be used in ye Convention every morning."[41] Ben Franklin himself seconded this substitute motion. So while Franklin's initial request was not officially acted upon, neither was it officially rejected.

> **DID YOU KNOW?**
> *Congress has opened every session in prayer from the first (September 1774) to the most recent?*

The spirit of the request was carried out, breaking the impasse. Representative Dayton of New Jersey reported that when the delegates met again on July 2, much of the acrimony was gone: "We assembled again; and . . . every unfriendly feeling had been expelled, and a spirit of conciliation had been cultivated."[42]

Within a week, on the 4th of July, the entire assembly worshiped together at the Reformed Calvinistic Lutheran Church in Philadelphia. While some difficulties continued to arise before the conclusion of the Convention's business in September, the delegates apparently never returned to the fruitless acrimony that had existed prior to June 28th.

While it is probably an exaggeration to say – as some have – that America began as the result of a prayer meeting in Philadelphia, Dr. Franklin's call for prayer did play a critical role in reminding the delegates at a critical time that without God's help, all their efforts would be in vain.

The First Amendment

When the Convention concluded, the hard job of getting the states to ratify this new document began. The first problem that surfaced was that many of the states, and even some of the delegates, would not agree to ratify the Constitution without a written Bill of Rights. Patrick Henry, Samuel Adams, and even Thomas Jefferson, who was thousands of miles away in France as our ambassador at the time, were among the many leaders of the founding era who insisted that the Constitution must clearly contain in writing those specific liberties the colonists were intent on preserving.

So Congress drafted and enacted the first ten amendments to the Constitution, also known as the Bill of Rights, which include the First Amendment with its two important religion clauses: "Congress shall make no law respecting an establishment of religion or prohibiting the free exercise thereof..."[43] These two clauses are referred to legally as the Establishment Clause and the Free Exercise Clause. The first is a prohibition and the second is a guarantee.

> *James Madison, the chief architect of the Bill of Rights (including the First Amendment), introduced a bill into the Virginia Legislature on October 31, 1785, "For Appointing Days of Public Fasting and Thanksgiving."*

The reader should note that this Amendment says absolutely nothing about "the separation of church and state." In fact, that phrase is found nowhere in the Constitution or in the Bill of Rights. It was a doctrine imposed by the United States Supreme Court in a decision interpreting the Establishment Clause in the mid-20th century.[44]

The founders' own understanding of the Establishment Clause does not support this modern view. What the founders themselves meant by "an establishment of religion" in the First Amendment was simply that there should be no officially established national church which citizens would be forced to attend, as there had been in England.[45] Dr. Robert Cord, author of *Separation of Church and State: Historical Fact and Current Fiction*, describes Madison's original draft of the religion clauses in the First Amendment:

> Madison's original wording of the Establishment of Religion Clause also supports my thesis concerning the separation of Church and the national State: "The Civil rights of none shall be abridged on account of religious belief or worship, *nor shall any national religion be established*, nor shall the full and

equal rights of Conscience be in any manner, or on any pretext, infringed."[46]

Furthermore, prior to the mid-20th century, the prohibition in the First Amendment referred only to the federal government and not to the states, some of whom in 1789 had an established, tax-payer supported church. Massachusetts, for example, had a state church (the Congregational Church) until 1833. It is clear that the founders did not intend, by this Amendment, to institute a state-sanctioned atheism (which means "no god"). Yet that is what today's secularists are now seeking to impose on our nation. In the words of one law professor, the Establishment Clause has been converted to a "search and destroy mission against any sneaky vestiges of religion left around."[47]

A Cautionary Note

As great as the Constitution is, and as much as it was influenced by the Bible and by the Godly men who wrote it, we must never put that document on the same level as the Bible. I am not comfortable with some of the exaggerated claims made by the Black Regiment during the Revolutionary War when they declared that the cause of America is the cause of Christ. I am more comfortable with the humility of President Abraham Lincoln when he pointed out during the Civil War that we should not so much ask whether the Lord is on our side, but rather, if we are on the Lord's side.

Consider the inferiority of the Constitution when it is compared to the Bible, God's eternal, unchanging Word:

> "In this nation of spiritual paradoxes, it is legal to . . . utter virtually any conceivable blasphemy in a public place; it is not legal, the federal courts have ruled, to mention God reverently in a classroom, on a football field or at a commencement ceremony as part of a public prayer."
>
> *TIME* Magazine

God did not author the Constitution of the United States. God authored His immortal Word; but the Constitution is mortal. Christians must be careful not to raise anything else to an equal status with Scripture.

The Constitution is not a source of Christian beliefs. Even though America's Christian heritage influenced the writing of the Constitution, that document was conceived by men, and some of them were not so noble.

The Constitution is based on compromises. The delegates realized that unless they compromised, they could not unite the colonies. The Constitution is not the document every delegate thought was best; it is the document they thought the colonies would adopt. In contrast, the Word of God is never compromised in any respect. God wrote His Word with no thought as to whether anyone would accept it. He wrote it because it is Truth.

The Constitution is man-enforced. If Christians could stand with attorneys representing the Christian Law Association in courtrooms throughout this nation, they would see that what is enforced in one courtroom is not always enforced in another. In fact, often there is no absolute standard at all. The standard is whatever the judge thinks at the time. That is always the problem when men are involved; but God always enforces His Word consistently.

The Constitution is man-interpreted. It only takes five of the nine Supreme Court Justices to change the entire interpretation of the Constitution. Robert Bork pointed out that the Supreme Court "found a right to abortion in the Constitution without explaining even once how that right could be derived from any constitutional materials, and came within one vote of finding a constitutional right to engage in homosexual conduct."[48] How can that happen? Presidents, with the advice and consent of the Senate, appoint new Justices who interpret the Constitution in new ways. As one Supreme Court Justice in the early 20th century noted, the Constitution is whatever the judges say it is.[49] In contrast, God's Word is stable. It never changes. But the Constitution is unstable and judges have placed it in a constant state of flux.

The Constitution provides for its own amendment. Nothing in the Constitution is absolutely sacred. Every bit of it can be changed, even to the people's detriment, if that is what a majority of the people desire. In fact, that is what seems to be going on today in many legislative bodies across America. Without a revival and a touch of God on our nation, the Constitution may look very different in a decade or two. On the other hand, even if people try to rewrite the Word of God, it cannot change because God's Word is unchangeable.

While American Christians must take great care to preserve the gifts of freedom and self-government that God has given us, we must realize that it is God who raises up and tears down nations according to His sovereignty. No Christian should ever equate America with the Kingdom of God.

Conclusion

We have seen that the tenth thing every Christian should know about the founding of America is that the Biblical understanding of the sinfulness of man was the guiding principle behind the United States Constitution. And it is that very Biblical principle that should serve as a caution to us when we consider the miracle that God has wrought among us.

Chapter 11

The Motivation for the Original Settling
of Most of the Colonies

*"Therefore we conclude that a man is justified by faith
without the deeds of the law."*
~ Romans 3:28

hen we look at the vast majority of the people who settled
America and who organized its government, there is one feature
that stands out more than any other, and that is their faith. These
were men and women of great accomplishment, great daring, and great moral
character. But above all they were people of great faith.

What exactly was it they believed in so strongly that they were willing to
give up everything else? It was the Gospel of Jesus Christ. We hear that phrase
so often that it is good to clarify exactly what we mean by this Gospel.
Gospel means "good news." But to understand the good news, we must first
come to grips with the bad news.

The vast majority of the early settlers and founders of this nation believed
in the Biblical concept of the depravity of human nature. Quoting from James
Madison in *Federalist #51*: "If men were angels," the three divisions of power
written into our Constitution would not have been necessary.[1] The drafters of
that document believed in both private and public confession of sin. For
example, on June 12, 1775, the Continental Congress proclaimed a day of fast-

ing and prayer and confession of sins throughout the land so that the Almighty might bless them.[2] The vast majority of our Founding Fathers believed strongly in the base nature of mankind and the need to ask God for forgiveness of sin.

Our founders believed in personal salvation. They believed that peace with God could only be found through faith in Jesus Christ. George Whitefield, the key evangelist of the Great Awakening, which united the colonies spiritually in preparation for independence, asked:

> Would you have peace with God? Away, then, to God through Jesus Christ, who has purchased peace; the Lord Jesus has shed his heart's blood for this. He died for this; he rose again for this; he ascended into the highest heaven, and is now interceding at the right hand of God.[3]

Even those Founding Fathers who were not professing Christians saw the importance of personal salvation. For example, Thomas Jefferson, who – based on his own writings – is not generally considered to have been a Bible-believing Christian, wrote in his *Notes on Locke and Shaftesbury*: "No man has the right to abandon the care of his salvation to another."[4]

> *"For all have sinned, and come short of the glory of God; . . . "*
>
> Romans 3:23

How does one achieve salvation? How does one receive it? The answer is simple – too simple for many: Through faith in Jesus Christ alone. Rev. Jonathan Edwards, the man God used to begin the Great Awakening that led directly to America becoming one nation under God, said: "We are justified only by faith in Christ and not by any manner of virtue or goodness of our own. . . . Christ alone performs the condition of our justification and salvation. . . . Christ suffered the punishment of sin, not as a private person, but as our surety."[5] Surety is a legal term in which one person agrees to pay the debts of another.

The vast majority of early settlers in this country believed that when a man or woman repented and confessed their sins and received salvation, it would show in their lives. "There are two things to do about the gospel: believe it and behave it,"[6] said Susannah Wesley, mother of John and Charles. The Wesley brothers played a key role in spreading Christianity throughout the New World, especially on the frontier. William Penn said, "True Godliness doesn't turn men out of the World, but enables them to live better in it, and excites their endeavors to mend it."[7]

Not only did these early American settlers "mend it," but they also shaped, molded and formed their world. Civic and church leaders were often the same people, and one had to be a Christian to hold public office in the early colonies.

God's laws were enacted in the early colonial legal codes as the law of the land. The New Haven Colony Charter of 1644 read: "The judicial laws of God, as they were delivered by Moses . . . [are to] be a rule to all the courts in this jurisdiction."[8] James Madison also attested to the fact that true faith would lead to holy living: "It is not the talking but the walking and the working person that is the true Christian."[9]

Our earliest settlers believed in the sovereignty of God, as did our Founding Fathers. Here is how President George Washington worded his belief in God's sovereignty in his Thanksgiving Proclamation of 1789: "[I]t is the duty of all nations to acknowledge the providence of the Almighty God, to obey his will, to be grateful for his benefits, and humbly to implore his protection and favor."[10]

> *"I have called on Thee for pardon and forgiveness of sins . . . accept and answer for the sake of Thy Dear Son, Jesus Christ our Lord, Amen."*
>
> From a book of prayers found among the papers of George Washington

Early Americans also believed in The Kingship of Christ. This was not merely a minor doctrine. Many settlers viewed the Lord as their only legitimate king or ruler. For example, in 1776, the small town of Ashfield, Massachusetts, passed this motion in a town meeting: "[W]e do not count any Governor but the Governor of the universe, and under him a States General to Consult with the rest of the united States for the Good of the Whole."[11] "We have no King but Jesus" was a rallying cry for American independence from England.

Many of the Puritan covenants – agreements for self-government wherein God was called upon as a witness, the true forerunners of our Constitution – submit the signers therein to God first and then to each other. Here is a well-worded example of this practice: "We . . . submit our persons, lives and estates unto our Lord Jesus Christ, the King of Kings, and Lord of Lords and to all those perfect and most absolute laws of his given us in his holy word."[12]

The early colonists believed their land was a gift from God. One of the representatives to the Constitutional Convention, New Jersey delegate William Livingston, said: "The land we possesses is the gift of heaven to our fathers and Divine Providence seems to have decreed it to our latest posterity."[13]

These early Americans believed in covenant living. This meant not only having a strong relationship between God and the individual, but also a bond of honor, responsibility, and accountability with each other. The Pilgrims described it this way: "We are knit together as a body in a most strict and sacred bond and covenant of the Lord."[14] Such covenant living is simply an extension of the communion of the saints, and it made the towns and small communities in the colonies much more than just a group of people living in the same area.

From Columbus to the Pilgrims, and from the Puritans to colonists of many different sects, virtually all of them believed in sharing the Gospel, in expanding the Kingdom of Christ, and in taking their faith to all those who did not know Jesus, including the Indians. Along with Columbus, many others saw it as their goal "to bear the light of Christ west to the heathen undiscovered lands."[15]

If you have come to realize in reading this book that you do not have what our forefathers saw as the most important thing of all, a saving knowledge of the Lord Jesus Christ, then I have great news for you. You can find peace with God here and now. The first step is to acknowledge your sins. The Ten Commandments are only the beginning of what God requires. We have all broken God's law, and we are all guilty. The verdict

> *"... Believe on the Lord Jesus Christ, and thou shalt be saved, ... "*
>
> Acts 16:31b

against all of us is based upon the fact that all of us have broken God's law; it does not depend upon any feelings of guilt on our part. Our remorse and our turning away from all immorality and sin is called repentance. Everyone who comes to God must come in humility, asking His forgiveness, knowing that none of us deserves it.

The good news, the "Gospel," is that God forgives everyone who comes to Him earnestly, not because of anything we have done, but only because of Jesus' death on the cross. This is the heart of the Gospel: God forgives us and erases our guilt and all our wrong doings because of Christ. On the cross, Jesus paid the penalty for our infractions. God, who is the lawgiver, the Judge, and the executioner, will not exact payment twice. If we accept Christ's death in our place, we go free. But not only does the Lord free us, He also adopts us into His own family, and declares His undying and eternal love and care for us.

If you have never accepted Jesus as your Savior and Lord, I invite you right now to pray:

> Dear Lord Jesus, I recognize that I am a sinner, incapable of saving my own soul. I recognize that my own "righteousness" is inadequate to earn me a place in heaven. I recognize that only by Your grace, only because You shed Your

own blood for sinners on the cross can anyone get to heaven. I place my trust in You. I ask You to come into my life and cleanse me from all unrighteousness. Please make me a new creation in You. Thank You for dying on the cross and rising again from the dead. In Your name I pray. Amen.

If you sincerely prayed that prayer, I encourage you to get a Bible and read it. I strongly recommend that you begin by reading the Gospels in the New Testament; for example, the Gospel of Mark and the Gospel of John.

One of the most important things for you to do after you join the family of God as a redeemed sinner is to find a good Bible-believing church. Attending such a church will bolster you in your newfound faith. There is no such thing as a "Lone Ranger Christian."

> *"O may we meet in Heaven, to which the merits of Jesus will carry those who love and serve Him."*
>
> Patrick Henry,
> letter to his sister after the death
> of her husband, 1786

I also recommend that you cultivate the habit of praying every day. Our nation's first President, George Washington – despite his busy life – found time to pray every day. His prayer life was legendary. Always remember that if you are too busy to pray, you are too busy.

If you prayed the sinner's prayer printed above, I want to congratulate you on your new life in Christ, which, you will find to be the most important decision of your entire life. Jesus once said that the kingdom of heaven was like a little yeast (leaven), working its way through the dough. It starts off very small, but as it works through the dough, it impacts the whole batch. So it is with the kingdom of God in a human life. It soon becomes the center of your life. And your life will never be the same (Matthew 13:33).

If we *truly* become God's man or woman, girl or boy – by asking for His forgiveness, by repenting from our sins and trusting in His finished work of salvation – from then on, we belong to Him for time and eternity. We do not rule our own lives anymore. We are now under a new jurisdiction, subjects of His eternal kingdom. We become heirs of the King of the Universe. We are now members of the royal family and should live lives worthy of the holy name "Christian." When we become part of the Kingdom, it is our joy to spread the good news of this Gospel to others and to expand the light into our dark world.

One day, we will meet in heaven all the sincere Pilgrims, Puritans, Baptists, Presbyterians, Dutch Reformed, Quakers, Anglicans, Methodists, and all those we have met in this book who founded this great nation – every one of them who *truly* knew the Lord. I look forward to meeting Gov. William Bradford, Gov. John Winthrop, Rev. Roger Williams, William Penn, Rev. George Whitefield, President George Washington, Sam Adams, and so many others. Those who truly made their peace with God through Christ our Savior are now in heaven, worshiping Jesus in person. One day we will join them. What an incredible day that will be!

Conclusion

We know from the word of God that America can be healed and our national conscience restored. II Chronicles 7:14 declares: "If my people, which are called by my name, shall humble themselves, and pray, and seek my face, and turn from their wicked ways; then will I hear from heaven, and will forgive their sin, and will heal their land." It starts with the people of God deciding to obey the Word of God. We must humble ourselves, pray, seek His face, and turn from our wicked ways. After that, God promises to hear us, to forgive us, and to heal our land.

Every person who reads this book faces a few key decisions.

1) Will you accept or reject Jesus Christ as your Savior?
2) After you have accepted Jesus Christ as your Savior, will you follow II Chronicles 7:14 and be part of the answer for our nation?

For the sake of the next generation, let us once again turn America back to God. That is what our Founding Fathers would have wanted, and we know God will reward our efforts toward that end.

My prayer is that God will raise up a new generation of Christian patriots in our time who will spread the Gospel of Jesus Christ and apply the truths of the Word of God to all facets of life, including politics, law, communications, business and every other aspect of our national life. Our nation began as a Christian nation. It began "in the name of God." It is high time we remember our national beginnings and recall once again the rich Judeo-Christian heritage that made America great! The hour is late, but it is not too late.

With God, all things are possible (Matthew 19:26).

Chapter Endnotes

Introduction

1. Alexis deTocqueville, *Democracy in America* (trans. Henry Reeve; Rev. Francis Bower; ed. Phillips Bradley; New York: Vintage Books, 1958), Vol. II, 6.

2. Gilbert K. Chesterton, "What I Saw in America" (New York: Dodd, Mead, 1922), quoted in Benjamin Hart, *Faith & Freedom: The Christian Roots of American Liberty* (San Bernardino, CA: Here's Life Publishers, 1988), 13.

3. Paul Johnson, *A History of the American People* (New York: HarperCollins*Publishers*, 1997), 3.

4. "Charter of Rhode Island and Providence Plantation" (1663), <http://yale.edu/lawweb/avalon/states/ri04.htm> (2002, spelling modernized).

5. "Instructions Issued by Queen Christina regarding the New Sweden Colony in 1642." Barry Liimakka; <http://members.home.net/finnsite/HXqueen.htm> (31 July 2000), quoted in *The Legal Alert* (Seminole, Fla.: Christian Law Association), October 2001, 3.

6. "Charter of Pennsylvania, 1681, granted to William Penn by King Charles II." *A Collection of Charters and Other Public Acts Relating to the Province of Pennsylvania* (Philadelphia: B. Franklin, 1740), 1, quoted in William J. Federer, *American's God and Country: Encyclopedia of Quotations* (St. Louis, MO: Amerisearch, Inc. 1994 / 2000), 502.

Chapter 1

1. George Bancroft, *History of the United States of America, From the Discovery of the Continent* (New York: D. Appleton and Company, 1890), Vol. I, 7.

2. William J. Federer, *America's God and Country: Encyclopedia of Quotations* (St. Louis, MO: Amerisearch, Inc., 1994 / 2000), 45.

3. Valerie Richardson, "Pre-Columbian PC: Berkeley seizes day for the 'indigenous,'" *The Washington Times*, 11 January 1992, A1.

4. Ibid., A5.

5. Quoted in George Grant, *The Last Crusader: The Untold Story of Christopher Columbus* (Wheaton, Ill.: Crossway Books, 1992), 117.

6. Russell Means, quoted in ibid.

7. Dwight D. Eisenhower, 14 June 1954, quoted in William J. Federer, "Public Papers of Dwight D. Eisenhower 1953-1961," United States Folder in *Library of Classics* (St. Louis, MO: Amerisearch, Inc., 2002), a CD-ROM.

8. Dwight D. Eisenhower, recorded for the "Back-to-God" Program of the American Legion, 20 February 1955, quoted in Federer, United States Folder, *Library of Classics*.

9. Christopher Columbus, *Journal*, 1942, quoted in Federer, United States Folder, *Library of Classics*.

10. *Compton's Pictured Encyclopedia and Fact-Index*, F. E. Compton & Company (Chicago et al: William Benton, Publisher, 1963), Vol. 8, 129.

11. John Eidsmoe, *Columbus & Cortez, Conquerors for Christ* (Green Forest, AR: New Leaf Press, 1992), 15.

12. Ibid., 16.

13. Samuel P. Huntington, "The West Unique, Not Universal," *Foreign Affairs* (Vol. 75, No. 6, November/December 1996), 30.

14. Grant, *The Last Crusader*, 47-48. It should be noted that the Emperor Constantine referenced here was the last emperor of the Byzantine Empire. He was not the famous Emperor Constantine who lived 1100 years earlier, and who gave his name to the City of Constantinople.

15. Eidsmoe, *Columbus & Cortez*, 55.

16. Christopher Columbus, *Book of Prophecies* (trans. Kay Brigham; Fort Lauderdale, FL: TSELF, Inc., 1991), 182-183.

17. Ibid., 23.

18. Marvin Lunenfeld, "Columbus, Christopher," *World Book Encyclopedia* (Chicago: World Book, Inc., 1997), Vol. 4, 858.

19. Kay Brigham, *Christopher Columbus: His life and discovery in the light of his prophecies* (Barcelona, Spain: CLIE, 1990), 19.

20. Christopher Columbus, letter to Luis de Sant Angel, 15 February 1493, quoted in

Eidsmoe, *Columbus and Cortez*, 86-87.

21. Bancroft, *A History of the United States*, Vol. I, 8.

22. Columbus, quoted in Eidsmoe, *Columbus & Cortez*, 90.

23. Ibid., 91.

24. Bancroft, *A History of the United States*, Vol. I, 11.

25. Desmond Wilcox, *Ten Who Dared* (Boston: Little, Brown and Company, 1977), 45-46.

26. "1492 Christopher Columbus," in Federer, United States Folder, *Library of Classics*.

Chapter 2

1. Interview with Paul Jehle, on location in Plymouth, MA, Coral Ridge Ministries-TV, Ft. Lauderdale, August 1989.

2. Cotton Mather, *The Great Works of Christ in America: Magnalia Christi Americana* (Edinburgh: The Banner of Truth Trust, 1702 / 1853 / 1979), Vol. 1, 46-47 (emphasis in original).

3. Ibid., 49 (emphasis in original).

4. Edward Winslow, quoted in William B. Sprague, "Annals of the American Pulpit," 1857, cited in Verna Hall, ed., *The Christian History of the Constitution of the United States of America* (San Francisco: Foundation for American Christian Education, 1960 / 1993), 184.

5. Jordan D. Fiore, ed., *Mourt's Relation: A Journal of the Pilgrims of Plymouth* (Plymouth, Mass: Plymouth Rock Foundation, 1985), 9.

6. Mather, *The Great Works of Christ in America*, Vol. I, 50 (emphasis in original).

7. Ibid., 47.

8. William Bradford, *Of Plymouth Plantation*, 1620-1647, edited and updated by Samuel Eliot Morison (New York: Alfred A. Knopf, 1952, 2001), 25.

9. *The World Almanac and Book of Facts 2001*, (Mahwah, NJ: World Almanac Books, 2001), 457 (emphasis in the original).

10. Paul Johnson, *A History of the American People* (New York: HarperCollins Publishers, 1997), 29.

11. Ibid., 29-30.

12. Declaration of Independence, 4 July 1776. *The World Almanac and Book of Facts 2001*, 459.

13. Interview with Dr. Robert Bartlett, on location at Plymouth, MA. Coral Ridge Ministries-TV, Ft. Lauderdale, FL, August, 1989.

14. Interview with Rev. Peter Marshall, on location at Plymouth, MA. Coral Ridge Ministries-TV, Ft. Lauderdale, FL, August, 1989.

Chapter 3

1. Cotton Mather, *The Great Works of Christ in America: Magnalia Christi America*na (Edinburgh: The Banner of Truth Trust, 1702 / 1853 / 1979), Vol. 1, 67 (emphasis in original).

2. Ibid., 70 (emphasis in original).

3. Ibid., 71.

4. George Bancroft, *History of the United States of America, From the Discovery of the Continent* (New York: D. Appleton and Company, 1859 / 1890), Vol. I, 228.

5. John Winthrop, "A Model of Christian Charity," 1630, *The Annals of America* (Chicago et al.: Encyclopedia Britannica, 1976), Vol. 1, 115.

6. Ibid.

7. Ibid.

8. Clarence B. Carson, *A Basic History of the United States, Volume I: The Colonial Experience 1607-1774* (Wadley, AL: American Textbook Committee, 1983 / 1987), 17.

9. Mather, *The Great Works of Christ in America*, Vol. 2, 98 (emphasis in original).

10. Rush H. Limbaugh III, *See, I Told You So* (New York et al: Pocket Star Books, Simon & Schuster Inc., 1993 / 1994), 81.

11. New England ministers meeting in Cambridge, *The Platform of Church-discipline,* also known as "The American Church Manual," 30 September 1648, Chapter XXIV. "Of the Civil Magistrate," quoted in Mather, *The Great Works of Christ,* Vol. 2, 201.

12. Ibid.

13. Ibid., 202.

14. Mather, *The Great Works of Christ in America*, Vol. 2, 207.

15. Ibid., 208.

16. Quoted in Verna Hall, ed., *The Christian History of the Constitution of the United States of America* (San Francisco: Foundation for American Christian Education, 1960 / 1993), 252.

17. Quoted in ibid., 249.

18. Ibid., 252.

19. Ibid.

20. Quoted in ibid., 272.

21. Quoted in ibid., 279.

22. Richard Frothingham, *The Rise of the Republic*, 1890, quoted in ibid., 287.

23. Catherine Drinker Bowen, *Miracle at Philadelphia: The Story of the Constitutional Convention May to September 1787* (Boston et al: An Atlantic Monthly Press Book, a division of Little, Brown and Company, 1966 / 1986), 151.

Chapter 4

1. Quoted in George Bancroft, *History of the United States of America, From the Discovery of the Continent* (New York: D. Appleton and Company, 1859 / 1890), Vol. 1, 250.

2. Os Guinness, *The Great Experiment* (Colorado Springs: NavPress, 2001), 63.

3. Ibid.

4. Bancroft, *History of the United States of America*, Vol. I, 251.

5. Ibid., 250.

6. Ibid.

7. Quoted in ibid., 178.

8. Ibid.

9. Roger Williams, quoted in Guinness, *The Great Experiment*, 64.

10. Roger Williams, letter to Gov. Endicott, John Winthrop's successor, 1651, quoted in Ibid., 66.

11. Quoted in Bancroft, *History of the United States of America*, Vol. I, 254.

12. Ibid.

13. Ibid.

14. Ibid., 254-255.

15. Roger Williams, "A Plea for Religious Liberty," (1644), <http://www.constitution.org/bcp/religlib.html> (31 January 2003).

16. Bancroft, *History of the United States of America*, Vol. I, 255.

17. William J. Federer, *America's God and Country: Encyclopedia of Quotations* (St. Louis, MO: Amerisearch, 2000), 238.

18. Text of *Concessions and Agreements* (1680), quoted in Catherine Owens Peare, *William Penn*, (Ann Arbor, Michigan: University of Michigan Press, 1956), 172-173. (emphasis in original).

19. Ibid., 173.

20. Peare, *William Penn*, 174.

21. Ibid., 275.

22. Letter from William Penn to Robert Turner, 5 March 1681, quoted in Bancroft, *History of the United States of America*, Vol. I, 553.

23. Letter from William Penn to the inhabitants of Pennsylvania, 8 April 1681, quoted in Bancroft, *History of the United States of America*, Vol. I, 553.

24. Peare, *William Penn*, 227.

25. Quoted in ibid., 434.

26. Ibid., 230.

27. Bancroft, *History of the United States of America*, Vol. I, 554.

28. Quoted in ibid.

29. Paul Johnson, *A History of the American People* (New York: HarperCollins *Publishers*, 1997), 66.

30. Ibid.

31. Bancroft, *History of the United States of America*, Vol. I, 553-554.

32. Johnson, *A History of the American People*, 59-60.

33. John Eidsmoe, *Christianity and the Constitution: The Faith of our Founding Fathers* (Grand Rapids, MI: Baker Book House, 1987), 18.

34. Abraham Kuyper, *You Can Do Greater Things Than Christ*, trans. Jan H. Boer (Jos, Nigeria: Institute of Church and Society, 1991), 74. This comes from the first volume of Kuyper's book, which was first published as *Pro Rege, of Het Koningschap van Christus* in 1911.

35. Loraine Boettner, *The Reformed Doctrine of Predestination* (Philadelphia: The Presbyterian and Reformed Publishing Company, 1975), 382.

36. Ibid., 382-383.

37. Quoted in ibid., 383.

38. Ibid.

39. Quoted in ibid.

40. E. W. Smith, *The Creed of Presbyterians*, p. 142, quoted in ibid., 389.

41. George Bancroft, quoted in Philip Schaff, *History of the Christian Church* (Peabody, MA: Hendrickson Publishers, 1892 / 1996), Vol. 8, 523.

42. Letter from John Adams to Thomas Jefferson, 28 June 1813, from Quincy, quoted in Guinness, *The Great Experiment*, 149-150.

Chapter 5

1. *The New-England Primer* (Boston: Edward Draper's Printing-Office, 1690 / 1777. Reprinted by David Barton, Aledo, TX: Wallbuilders, 1991), pages unnumbered. However, if one were to number the title page beginning after David Barton's introduction, this entry would be found on page 16.

2. John Eidsmoe, *Christianity and the Constitution: The Faith of our Founding Fathers* (Grand Rapids, MI: Baker Book House, 1987), 22.

3. Transcript of a Coral Ridge Ministries-TV interview with David Barton, 10 October 2002.

4. George Bancroft, *History of the United States of America, From the Discovery of the Continent* (New York: D. Appleton and Company, 1859 / 1890), Vol. I, 316-317.

5. Ibid., 316.

6. *The New-England Primer*, page 10 (using the criterion described in footnote 1).

7. Ibid., page 11 (using the criterion described in footnote 1).

8. William J. Federer, *America's God and Country: Encyclopedia of Quotations* (St. Louis, MO: Amerisearch, Inc., 1994 / 2000), 158.

9. The Northwest Ordinance, quoted in *The Annals of America* (Chicago, et. al: Encyclopedia Britannica, Inc., 1976), Vol. 3, 194-195.

10. *The Constitutions of All the United States According to the Latest Amendments* (Lexington, KY: Thomas T. Skillman, 1817), 389, as quoted in Federer, *America's God and Country*, 451.

11. Cotton Mather, *The Great Works of Christ in America: Magnalia Christi Americana* (Edinburgh: The Banner of Truth Trust, 1702 / 1853 / 1979), Vol. II, 8 (emphasis in original).

12. Ibid., 9.

13. Ibid. See also Paul Johnson, *A History of the American People* (New York:

HarperCollinsPublishers, 1997), 53.

14. Mather, T*he Great Works of Christ in America*, Vol. II, 10.

15. Ibid..

16. Ibid.

17. Rules for Harvard University, 1643, from "New England's First Fruits," *The Annals of America*, Vol. 1, 176 (emphasis in original).

18. Ibid., 176-177.

19. Ibid., 177.

20. Federer, *America's God and Country*, 281-282.

21. Mather, *The Great Works of Christ in America*, Vol. II, 14.

22. Ibid., 22 (emphasis in original).

23. To give an example of how liberal Harvard Divinity School has become, consider the following selection from Dr. D. James Kennedy and Jerry Newcombe in their book on the assault against Christianity in America today, *The Gates of Hell Shall Not Prevail:*

> On the day after Easter 1994, the perceptive syndicated columnist, Don Feder, who is an Orthodox Jew, wrote about Harvard Divinity School. He points out how far this school is from its Puritan roots:
>
>> Instead of singing hymns, they're sitting in the lotus position, chanting 'omm' at America's oldest school of theology. The Nave's [student newsletter] calendar reminds students that March 20 is Spring Ohigon, 'a special time to listen to the Buddha and meditate on the perfection of enlightenment' . . . There's no mention of Palm Sunday or Passover, reflecting their insignificance at an institution where all is venerated, save Western religion.
>
> Feder has a friend studying there who told him that at Harvard Divinity School, "all religions are equal except Christianity, which is very bad, and Judaism, which loses points *where it intersects with Christianity.*" Feder refers to it as a "poison-ivy" school! Source: D. James Kennedy and Jerry Newcombe, *The Gates of Hell Shall Not Prevail* (Nashville: Thomas Nelson, 1996), 148-149, (emphasis in original).

24. Mather, *The Great Works of Christ in America*, Vol. II, 27.

25. "New England's First Fruits," 1643, quoted in *The Annals of America*, Vol. 1, 175.

26. D. James Kennedy and Jerry Newcombe, *What If Jesus Had Never Been Born?* (Nashville: Thomas Nelson, 1994), 52.

27. William and Mary, College of, entry in *The World Book Encyclopedia* (Chicago, et al.: World Book, Inc., 1997), Vol. 21, 311.

28. "The Statutes of the College of William and Mary," *The Annals of America*, Vol. 1, 371.

29. Bancroft, *History of the United States,* Vol. 1, 361

30. Yale, Elihu, entry in *World Book Encyclopedia* (Chicago et al.: World Book, Inc., 1997), Vol. 21, 551.

31. "Regulations at Yale College," 1745, *The Annals of America,* Vol. 1, 464.

32. Ibid., 466.

33. Quoted in Paul Lee Tan, *Encyclopedia of 7,700 Illustrations: Signs of the Times* (Rockville, MD: Assurance Publishers, 1984), 158.

34. Quoted in John Irving, *A Discourse of the Advantages of Classical Learning* (New York: G. & C. & H. Carvill, 1830), 141-143, in Federer, *America's God and Country,* 337-338.

35. Princeton University. Stephen K. McDowell and Mark A. Beliles, *America's Providential History* (Charlottesville, VA: Providence Press, 1988), 93, as quoted in Federer, *America's God and Country,* 519.

36. Eidsmoe, *Christianity and the Constitution,* 81.

37. Bancroft, *History of the United States,* Vol. IV, 33.

38. Robert Flood, *Men Who Shaped America* (Chicago: Moody Press, 1976), 41.

39. Quoted in ibid., 43.

40. Entry on "Dartmouth," *World Book Encyclopedia* (Chicago et al.: World Book, Inc., a Scott Fetter company, 1997) Vol. 5, 39.

Chapter 6

1. Paul Johnson, *A History of the American People* (New York: HarperCollins*Publishers,* 1997), 204.

2. Quoted in *The Annals of America* (Chicago, et al.: Encyclopedia Britannica, 1976), Vol. 1, 172.

3. Johnson, *A History of the American People,* 115.

4. Ibid., 204.

5. Ibid., 110.

6. Ibid., 110-111.

7. Tryon Edwards, *The New Dictionary of Thoughts – A Cyclopedia of Quotations* (Garden City, NY: Hanover House 1852, The Standard Book Company, 1963), 91, quoted in William J. Federer, *America's God and Country: Encyclopedia of Quotations* (St. Louis, MO:

Amerisearch, 2000), 225.

8. Federer, *America's God and Country*, 223.

9. Robert Flood, *Men Who Shaped America* (Chicago: Moody Press, 1976), 49.

10. Quoted in William Warren Sweet, *The Story of Religion in America* (New York: Harper, 1950), 130, in Flood, *Men Who Shaped America*, 50.

11. Quoted in Peter Marshall and David Manuel, *The Light and the Glory* (Old Tappan, NJ: Fleming H. Revell Company, 1977), 242-243.

12. Ibid., 243.

13. Flood, *Men Who Shaped America*, 51-52.

14. Ibid., 50.

15. Johnson, A History of the American People, 113.

16. Benjamin Franklin, *The Autobiography of Benjamin Franklin: Poor Richard's Almanac and Other Papers* (Reading, PA: The Spencer Press, 1936), 133.

17. Ibid., 136 (emphasis in original).

18. Ibid., 137.

19. In J. I. Packer, "The Startling Puritan" (Carol Stream, IL: Christian History), Vol. XII, No. 2, Issue 38, p. 40, quoted in Federer, *America's God and Country*, 685.

20. A letter from Sarah Edwards to her brother, quoted in Federer, *America's God and Country*, 685-686.

21. Johnson, *A History of the American People*, 114.

22. Franklin, *Autobiography*, 133.

23. Russell T. Hitt, ed., *Heroic Colonial Christians* (Philadelphia: J. B. Lippincott Co., 1966), 198, quoted in Marshall and Manuel, *The Light and the Glory*, 246.

24. Johnson, *A History of the American People*, 307.

25. Ellis Sandoz, *A Government of Laws: Political Theory, Religion, and the American Founding* (Baton Rouge and London: Louisiana State University Press, 1990), 147.

26. George Bancroft, *History of the United States of America, From the Discovery of the Continent* (New York: D. Appleton and Company, 1890), Vol. IV, 25.

27. Ibid., 20.

28. Quoted in Federer, *America's God and Country*, 637.

29. Bancroft, *History of the United States*, Vol. IV, 73.

30. Quoted in ibid., 20.

31. Stephen J. Keillor, *This Rebellious House* (Downers Grove, IL: IVP, 1996), 89.

32. Bancroft, *History of the United States*, Vol. IV, 43-44.

33. Quoted in ibid., 46.

34. Quoted in ibid., 92.

35. Frank S. Mead, *The Encyclopedia of Religious Quotations* (Old Tappan, NJ: Fleming H. Revell Company, 1965), 150.

36. Declaration of Independence, Bruce Frohnen, ed., *The American Republic: Primary Sources* (Indianapolis: Liberty Fund, 2002), 190.

37. Johnson, *A History of the American People*, 115.

38. Ibid., 116.

39. Ibid.

40. Ibid., 116-117.

Chapter 7

1. Franklin P. Cole, *They Preached Liberty: An anthology of timely quotations from New England ministers of the American Revolution on the subject of Liberty: Its source, nature, obligations, types, and blessings* (Ft. Lauderdale: Coral Ridge Ministries, undated, c. 1985).

2. Ibid., 115.

3. George Bancroft, *History of the United States of America, From the Discovery of the Continent* (New York: D. Appleton and Company, 1890), Vol. IV, 95.

4. George Whitefield, October 12, 1740, in Peter Gomes, "George Whitefield in the Old Colony: 1740," L. D. Geller, ed., *They Knew They Were Pilgrims* (New York: Poseidon Books, Inc., 1971), 93, quoted in Peter Marshall and David Manuel, *The Light and the Glory* (Old Tappan, NJ: Fleming H. Revell Company, 1977), 249.

5. In Clinton Rossiter, *Seedtime of the Republic* (New York: Harcourt, Brace & World, Inc., 1953), 241, quoted in William J. Federer, *America's God and Country: Encyclopedia of Quotations* (St. Louis, MO: Amerisearch, Inc., 1994 / 2000), 436.

6. John C. Fitzpatrick, ed., *The Writings of Washington*, Vol. XII, (Washington, D.C.: U.S. Government Printing Office, 1932), 343.

7. Phillips Payson, Massachusetts Election Sermon of 1778.
<http://www.lexrex.com/informed/otherdocuments/sermons/mass_sermon.htm>
(31 January 2003).

8. Cole, *They Preached Liberty*, 15.

9. Ibid., 16.

10. Baron de Charles Louis de Secondat Montesquieu, in Book XXIV of *The Spirit of Laws*, quoted in William J. Federer, *America's God and Country*, 454.

11. Donald S. Lutz, *The Origins of American Constitutionalism*, (Baton Rouge: Louisiana State University Press, 1988), 140-142.

12. Cole, *They Preached Liberty*, 16-17.

13. Ibid., 20.

14. Ibid., 21.

15. Quoted in Os Guinness, *The Great Experiment* (Colorado Springs: NavPress, 2001), 116.

16. Bancroft, *History of the United States*, Vol. IV, 14.

17. Quoted in Guinness, *The Great Experiment*, 116.

18. Quoted in ibid.

19. Quoted in ibid., 118.

20. Jonathan Mayhew, "A Discourse Concerning Unlimited Submission and Non-Resistance to the Higher Powers," 1750. <http://www.founding.com/library/lbody.cfm?id=230&parent=52> (emphasis in original).

21. Cole, *They Preached Liberty*, 25.

22. Jonathan Mayhew, to the Council and House of Representatives in Colonial New England, 1749, quoted in Verna M. Hall, ed., *The Christian History of the Constitution of the United States of America* (San Francisco: Foundation for American Christian Education, 1960 / 1993), 374-375. (Note: This reference is from Rev. Mayhew's preface to this published sermon.)

23. Ibid., 374-375.

24. Mayhew, "A Discourse Concerning Unlimited Submission and Non-Resistance to the Higher Powers," quoted in Hall, ed., *The Christian History of the Constitution*.

25. Cole, *They Preached Liberty*, 52.

26. Samuel West, Boston, 1776, in John Wingate Thornton, *The Pulpit of the American Revolution* (Boston: D. Lothrop & Co., 1876), 311, quoted in Marshall and Manuel, *The Light and the Glory*, 296-297.

27. Quoted in David Barton, *Original Intent* (Aledo, TX: WallBuilder Press, 1996), 104.

28. Bancroft, *History of the United States of America*, Vol. IV, 318.

29. Federer, *America's God and Country,* 460.

30. Richard Frothingham, *Rise of the Republic of the United States* (Boston: Little, Brown & Co., 1872), 393.

31. Bancroft, *History of the United States of America,* Vol. IV, 154.

32. Ibid., 155.

33. Ibid.

34. Ibid., 156.

35. Cole, *They Preached Liberty,* 112 (emphasis in original).

36. Quoted in Bancroft, *History of the United States of America,* Vol. IV, 157.

37. Ibid., 158.

38. Ibid., 164.

39. Quoted in Guinness, *The Great Experiment,* 116.

Chapter 8

1. Benjamin Hart, *Faith & Freedom: The Christian Roots of American Liberty* (San Bernardino, CA: Here's Life Publishers, 1988), 227.

2. Quoted in George Bancroft, *History of the United States of America, From the Discovery of the Continent* (New York: D. Appleton and Company, 1890), Vol. IV, 78.

3. Ibid., 209.

4. Quoted in ibid.

5. Ibid., 210-211.

6. Entry on George Washington, *Compton's Pictured Encyclopedia and Fact-Index* (Chicago et al: F.E. Compton Co., 1965), Vol. 15, 22.

7. Quoted in Bancroft, *History of the United States of America,* Vol. IV, 212.

8. John Eidsmoe, *Christianity and the Constitution: The Faith of our Founding Fathers* (Grand Rapids, MI: Baker Book House, 1987), 114, footnote 1.

9. Paul Johnson, *A History of the American People* (New York: HarperCollins*Publishers,* 1997), 205.

10. Steve Keillor, *This Rebellious House* (Downers Grove, IL: IVP, 1996), 51.

11. Eidsmoe, *Christianity and the Constitution,* 130.

12. William J. Federer, *America's God and Country* (St. Louis, MO: Amerisearch, Inc., 1994 / 2000), 656-658.

13. Bancroft, *History of the United States of America*, Vol. IV, 330.

14. Jared Sparks, ed., *The Writings of George Washington*, 12 vols. (Boston: American Stationer's Company, 1837, NY: F. Andrew's, 1834-1847), Vol. III, 491, as quoted in Eidsmoe, *Christianity and the Constitution*, 116.

15. George Washington, *Writings* (1932), Vol. XV, p. 55, from his speech to the Delaware Indian Chiefs on May 12, 1779, quoted in David Barton, *Original Intent* (Aledo, TX: Wallbuilders, 1996), 168.

16. John Clement Fitzpatrick, ed., *The Writings of George Washington, from the Original Manuscript Sources 1749-1799*, 39 vols. (Washington, D.C.: United States Government Printing Office, 1931-1944), Vol. XX, pp. 94-95.

17. *The Annals of America* (Chicago et al: Encyclopedia Britannica, 1976), Vol. 3, 345.

18. *Annals of Congress, 1789-1791* (Washington, D.C: Gales & Seaton, 1843), Vol. I, 25, as quoted in Federer, *America's God and Country*, 650. ("Resolved, That after the oath shall have been administered to the President, he, attended by the Vice President, and the members of the Senate, and House of Representatives, proceed to St. Paul's Chapel, to hear divine service, to be performed by the Chaplain of Congress already appointed.")

19. "Washington's Farewell Address," reproduced in *Compton's Pictured Encyclopedia and Fact-Index*, Vol. 15, 26.

20. Bancroft, *History of the United States of America*, Vol. IV, 34.

21. Ibid., Vol. III, 77.

22. John C. Miller, *Sam Adams: Pioneer in Propaganda* (Stanford, CA: Stanford University Press, 1936 /1960), 85, as quoted in Eidsmoe, *Christianity and the Constitution*, 248.

23. Ibid., 251.

24. Sam Adams, *Boston Gazette*, 24 August 1772; 2 November 1772, quoted in Eidsmoe, *Christianity and the Constitution*, 253.

25. *The Annals of America*, Vol. 2, 218-219.

26. Robert Flood, *Men Who Shaped America* (Chicago: Moody Press, 1976), 35-36.

27. *The Annals of America*, Vol. 2, 217.

28. Bancroft, *History of the United States of America*, Vol. IV, 23.

29. Samuel Adams, 1776, statement made while the Declaration of Independence was being signed. Charles E. Kistler, *This Nation Under God* (Boston: Richard G. Badger, The Gorham Press, 1924), 71, as quoted in Federer, *America's God and Country*, 143.

30. Quoted in Eidsmoe, *Christianity and the Constitution*, 255.

31. Johnson, *A History of the American People*, 145.

32. Bancroft, *History of the United States of America*, Vol. IV, 145.

33. *The Annals of America*, Vol. 2, 322-333.

34. Norine Dickson Campbell, *Patrick Henry - Patriot and Statesman* (Old Greenwich, CT: Devin Adair, 1969 / 1975), 417, quoted in Eidsmoe, *Christianity and the Constitution*, 314.

35. Stephen Abbott Northrop, D.D., *A Cloud of Witnesses* (Portland, Oregon: American Heritage Ministries, 1987), 227, quoted in William J. Federer "American Quotations" in William J. Federer, *Library of Classics* (St. Louis, MO: Amerisearch, Inc., 2002), a CD-ROM.

36. 20 November 1798, a Certified Copy of "Last Will and Testament of Patrick Henry," Patrick Henry Memorial Foundation, Red Hill, Brookneal, Virginia, in Henry, ed., *Patrick Henry - Life, Correspondence and Speeches*, Vol. II, 631, as quoted in Federer, *Library of Classics*.

Chapter 9

1. Quoted in George Bancroft, *History of the United States of America, From the Discovery of the Continent* (New York: D. Appleton and Company, 1890), Vol. IV, 64.

2. Charles Francis Adams, ed., *Letters of John Adams - Addressed To His Wife* (Boston: Charles C. Little and James Brown, 1841), Vol. I, 23-24.

3. Quoted in Verna Hall, ed., *The Christian History of the Constitution of the United States of America* (San Francisco: Foundation for American Christian Education, 1960 / 1993), 2.

4. Kenneth L. Woodward with David Gates, "How the Bible Made America: Since the Puritans and the pioneers, through wars and social conflicts, a sense of Biblical mission has united us, divided us and shaped our national destiny," *Newsweek*, 27 December 1982, 44.

5. Time, 25 May 1987.

6. Donald S. Lutz, *The Origins of American Constitutionalism*, (Baton Rouge: Louisiana State University Press, 1988), 121.

7. Bancroft, *History of the United States of America*, Vol. IV, 196.

8. Ibid., 197.

9. Loraine Boettner, *The Reformed Doctrine of Predestination* (Philadelphia: The Presbyterian and Reformed Publishing Company, 1975), 387.

10. "Mecklenburg County, Declaration of Independence," 20 May 1775. Raleigh (North Carolina) Register, 30 April 1819. Charles W. Eliot, LL.D., ed., *American Historical Documents 1000-1904* (New York: P.F. Collier & Son Company, The Harvard Classics, 1910), Vol. 43, 166.

11. N. S. McFetridge, *Calvinism in History*, 85-88, quoted in Boettner, *The Reformed Doctrine of Predestination*, 388.

12. "Declaration of Independence," *1998 World Almanac and Book of Facts* (Mahwah, NJ: World Almanac Books, 1998), 513.

13. Lutz, *The Origins of American Constitutionalism*, 115, discussing the Constitution of South Carolina – 26 March 1776.
<http://www.yale.edu/lawweb/avalon/states/sc01.htm> (31 January 2003).

14. Bancroft, *History of the United States of America*, Vol. IV, 444.

15. Ibid.

16. John Eidsmoe, *Christianity and the Constitution* (Grand Rapids: Baker Book House), 51.

17. David Barton, in D. James Kennedy, "What if Jesus Had Never Been Born?" (Ft. Lauderdale, FL: Coral Ridge Ministries-TV, 25 December 2002), a television special.

18. Eidsmoe, *Christianity and the Constitution*, 52.

19. Quoted in Verna Hall, ed., *The Christian History of the Constitution of the United States of America* (San Francisco: Foundation for American Christian Education, 1960 / 1993), 138.

20. "How the Founders built a nation on religion, philosophy." Review by Will Morrisey of Michael Novak's *On Two Wings: Humble Faith and Common Sense at the American Founding*, 28 January- 3 February 2002 National Weekly Edition, *The Washington Times*, 28.

21. Eidsmoe, *Christianity and the Constitution*, 54.

22. Frederick R. Coudert's special introduction to "The Spirit of Laws" (Colonial Press, 1900) in Hall, ed., *The Christian History of the Constitution*, 133.

23. Ibid., 134.

24. Sir James Mackintosh, *The Miscellaneous Works*, 1851, in Hall, ed., *The Christian History of the Constitution*, 244.

25. John Locke, *The Reasonableness of Christianity*, 1695, in Hall, ed., *The Christian History of the Constitution*, XIII.

26. John Locke, *Some Thoughts Concerning Reading and Study*, 1689, in Hall, ed., *The Christian History of the Constitution*, 37.

27. Lutz, *The Origins of American Constitutionalism*, 68, ftnt. 16.

28. Sir William Blackstone, *Commentaries on the Laws of England*, 3 Volumes (Philadelphia: J. B. Lippincott and Co., 1879), Vol. II, 59.

29. Chief Justice Roy S. Moore, *Our Legal Heritage* (Montgomery, AL: The Administrative Office of Courts, June 2001), 10.

30. Quoted in ibid., 8.

31. Quoted in ibid., 10.

32. Hebert W. Titus, *God, Man, and Law: The Biblical Principles* (Oak Brook, IL: Institute in Basic Life Principles, 1994), 41.

33. "Declaration of Independence," 4 July 1776, *The World Almanac and Book of Facts: 1998*, 512-513.

34. *Gulf, C. & S. F. Ry. Co. v. Ellis* (1897, US), 165 U.S. 150, 159, 17 S.Ct. 255.

35. "Declaration of Independence," 4 July 1776, *The World Almanac*, 512-513 (emphasis added).

36. Quoted in *Titus, God, Man, and Law*, 42.

37. Quoted in ibid. (emphasis added).

38. Quoted in ibid., 43.

39. Quoted in ibid., 42.

40. Quoted in ibid., 43.

41. Quoted in ibid., 44.

42. Quoted in ibid., 43.

43. Quoted in ibid., 44.

44. "Declaration of Independence," *1998 World Almanac*, 513.

45. George Mason "The Virginia Declaration of Rights," Sec. I, *National Archives and Records Administration*. <http://www.nara.gov/exhall/charters/billrights/virginia.html>(9 July 2001).

46. Sir William Blackstone, "Commentaries on the Laws of England: Book the First, of the Rights of Persons; Chapter the First, of the Absolute Rights Of Individuals." 1765. *The Claremont Institute*. <http://www.founding.com/library/lbody.cfm?id=542&parent=539> (31 January 2003).

47. Ibid.

48. John Locke, "An Essay Concerning the True Original, Extent, and End of Civil Government." 1690. *The Constitution Society*. <http://www.constitution.org/jl/2ndtreat.txt> (31 January 2003).

49. Quoted in *Titus, God, Man, and Law*, 43.

50. Ibid.

51. "Declaration of Independence," *1998 World Almanac*, 513.

52. Bancroft, *History of the United States of America*, Vol. IV, 442.

53. Paul Johnson, *A History of the American People* (New York: HarperCollins*Publishers*, 1997), 204-205.

Chapter 10

1. "How the Founders built a nation on religion, philosophy." 28 Jan. – 3 Feb. 2002 National Weekly Edition, *The Washington Times*, 28.

2. Transcript from a Coral Ridge Ministries-TV interview with William J. Federer on location in St. Louis, 10 July 2002.

3. Donald S. Lutz, *The Origins of American Constitutionalism* (Baton Rouge: Louisiana State University Press, 1988), 137.

4. Bishop Meade, *Old Churches, Ministers and Families of Virginia* (1872), quoted in John Eidsmoe, *Christianity and the Constitution: The Faith of our Founding Fathers* (Grand Rapids, MI: Baker Book House, 1987), 96.

5. James Madison, "Memorial and Remonstrance against Religious Assessments," 1785, quoted in Bruce Frohnen, ed., *The American Republic: Primary Sources* (Indianapolis: Liberty Fund, 2002), 328.

6. Eidsmoe, *Christianity and the Constitution*, 89.

7. Alexander Hamilton, James Madison, and John Jay, *The Federalist Papers*, with introduction by Clinton Rossiter (New York, et al: A Mentor Book from New American Library, 1961), 80.

8. Ibid., 301.

9. Eidsmoe, *Christianity and the Constitution*, 101.

10. Quoted in Catherine Drinker Bowen, *Miracle at Philadelphia: The Story of the Constitutional Convention May to September 1787* (Boston et al.: An Atlantic Monthly Press Book, a division of Little, Brown and Company, 1966 / 1986), 61.

11. Quoted in ibid., 138.

12. M.E. Bradford, *Religion & The Framers: The Biographical Evidence* (Marlborough, NH: The Plymouth Rock Foundation, 1991), 8.

13. Alexander Hamilton, 16-21 April 1802 letter to James Bayard. Claude G. Bowers, *Jefferson and Hamilton: The Struggle for Democracy in America* (Boston: Houghton Mifflin Co., 1925 / 1937), 40, quoted in William J. Federer, *America's God and Country* (St. Louis, MO: Amerisearch, Inc., 1994 / 2000), 274.

14. Hamilton, Madison, and Jay, *The Federalist Papers*, 59.

15. Ibid., 110.

16. Ibid., 346.

17. Ibid., 152 (emphasis in original).

18. Ibid., 313-314.

19. Quoted in Michael Kammen, ed., *The Origins of the American History: A Documentary History* (New York: Penguin Books, 1986), xiv.

20. Hamilton, Madison, and Jay, *The Federalist Papers*, 100.

21. Quoted in George Bancroft, *History of the United States of America, From the Discovery of the Continent* (New York: D. Appleton and Company, 1890), Vol. IV, 345.

22. Hamilton, Madison, and Jay, *The Federalist Papers*, 81.

23. Ibid., 83.

24. Montesquieu, "Spirit of Laws." Vol. I., page 186, quoted in ibid., 466, ftnt.

25. Hamilton, Madison, and Jay, *The Federalist Papers*, 467.

26. Rev. Samuel Cooper, "A Sermon on the Day of the Commencement of the Constitution," 25 October 1780.
<http://www.founding.com/library/lbody.cfm?id=486&parent=52> (31 January 2003).

27. Ibid.

28. John Adams, 11 October 1798. Letter to the officers of the First Brigade of the Third Division of the Militia of Massachusetts. Charles Francis Adams, ed., *The Works of John Adams – Second President of the United States: with a Life of the Author, Notes, and Illustration* (Boston: Little, Brown, & Co., 1854), Vol. IX, 228-229, quoted in William J. Bennett, *Our Sacred Honor* (Nashville: Broadman & Holman, 1997), 370.

29. Eidsmoe, *Christianity and the Constitution*, 43.

30. Hamilton, Madison, and Jay, *The Federalist Papers*, 188-189.

31. "Articles of Confederation," quoted in Bruce Frohnen, ed., *The American Republic: Primary Sources* (Indianapolis: Liberty Fund, 2002), 204

32. Quoted in Christine F. Hart, *One Nation Under God* (NJ: American Tract Society, reprinted by Gospel Tract Society, Inc., undated), 2, as quoted in Federer, *America's God and Country*, 273.

33. Quoted in Kammen, ed., *The Origins of the American History*, 54 (emphasis in original).

34. Washington to Lafayette, 7 February 1788, in Bowen, *Miracle at Philadelphia*, xvii.

35. Hamilton, Madison, and Jay, *The Federalist Papers*, 230-231.

36. Bowen, *Miracle at Philadelphia*, 86.

37. Ibid., 127.

38. Benjamin Franklin, 28 June 1787. James Madison, *Notes of Debates in the Federal Convention of 1787*. Gaillard Hunt and James B. Scott, ed., *The Debates in the Federal Convention of 1787 Which Framed the Constitution of the United States of America, reported by James Madison* (New York: Oxford University Press, 1920), 181-182, as quoted in Federer, *America's God and Country*, 248-249.

39. E.C. M'Guire, *The Religious Opinions and Character of Washington* (NY: Harper & Brothers, 1836), 151, as quoted in Federer, *America's God and Country*, 249.

40. Eidsmoe, *Christianity and the Constitution*, 209.

41. Benjamin Franklin, 28 June 1787. *James Madison, Notes of Debates in the Federal Convention of 1787* (New York: W.W. Norton & Co., 1787 / 1987), 210-211, as quoted in Federer, *America's God and Country*, 248-249.

42. M'Guire, *The Religious Opinions and Character of Washington*, 152, as quoted in ibid., 249.

43. U.S. Constitution, Amendment I, as quoted in Frohnen, ed., *The American Republic*, 349.

44. *Everson v. Board of Education*, 330 U.S. 1 (1947). The phrase "separation of church and state," as currently applied to the Establishment Clause, is taken from a private letter written in 1802 by Thomas Jefferson, who was in France when the Constitution and the First Amendment were written. Jefferson's letter was written thirteen years after the First Amendment was adopted. Furthermore, he likely knew that this phrase had first been penned by Roger Williams of Rhode Island who intended it to mean that the church must be protected from government control, not the other way around. In 1947, the Supreme Court for the first time ruled that the Establishment Clause should be applied to the states as well as to the federal government, and also that the "wall of separation" meant the strict separation of church and state.

45. See Debate over First Amendment Language in Frohnen, ed., *The American Republic*, 348-349.

46. Robert Cord, *Separation of Church and State: Historical Fact and Current Fiction* (New York: Lambeth Press, 1982), 7 (emphasis in original).

47. TV interview with Lynn Buzzard, conducted by Jerry Newcombe, August, 1987 in

Ft. Lauderdale for The Constitution in Crisis, 21 September 1987 edition of The Coral Ridge Hour.

48. Robert H. Bork, *The Tempting of America: The Political Seduction of the Law* (New York: A Touchstone Book, Simon & Schuster, 1990), 8-9.

49. Charles Evans Hughes 1907. (Hughes later served as a Justice on the U.S. Supreme Court). Gorton Carruth and Eugene Ehrich, *The Harper Book of American Quotations* (New York: Harper & Row, Publishers, 1988), 157.

Chapter 11

1. Alexander Hamilton, James Madison, and John Jay, *The Federalist Papers*, with introduction by Clinton Rossiter (New York, et al: A Mentor Book from New American Library, 1961), 322.

2. William J. Federer, *America's God and Country: Encyclopedia of Quotations* (St. Louis, MO: Amerisearch, Inc. 1994 / 2000), 139.

3. Quoted in J. I. Packer, *The Startling Puritan* (Carol Stream, IL: Christian History), Vol. XII, No. 2, Issue 38, p. 39, in ibid., 685.

4. Gorton Carruth and Eugene Ehrich, *The Harper Book of American Quotations* (New York: Harper & Row, Publishers, 1988), 492.

5. Ibid., 488.

6. Michael Reagan and Bob Phillips, *The All-American Quote Book* (Eugene, OR: Harvest House Publishers, 1995), 135.

7. Federer, *America's God and Country*, 500.

8. "Charter of New Haven Colony," 3 April 1644. John Fiske, *The Beginnings of New England* (Boston: Houghton, Mifflin & Co., 1898), 136, as quoted in Federer, *America's God and Country*, 472.

9. William C. Rives, *Biography of James Madison*, Vol. I, 33-34. Stephen Abbott Northrop, D.D., *A Cloud of Witnesses* (Portland, OR: American Heritage Ministries, 1987; Mantle Ministries, 228 Still Ridge, Bulverde, Texas), 307, as quoted in Federer, *America's God and Country*, 413.

10. George Washington, "Proclamation of a National Day of Thanksgiving," 3 October 1789. Jared Sparks, ed., *The Writings of George Washington*, Twelve Volumes (Boston: American Stationer's Company, 1837, NY: F. Andrew's, 1834-1847), Vol. XII, 119, as quoted in David Barton, *Original Intent* (Aledo ,TX: WallBuilder Press, 1996), 115.

11. Catherine Drinker Bowen, *Miracle at Philadelphia: The Story of the Constitutional*

Convention May to September 1787 (Boston et al.: An Atlantic Monthly Press Book, a division of Little, Brown and Company, 1966 / 1986), 11 (adapted into modern English by me).

12. David J. Brewer, *The United States: A Christian Nation* (Smyrna, GA: American Vision, 1905 / 1996), 16.

13. Federer, *America's God and Country*, 395.

14. Letter from John Robinson and William Brewster to Edwin Sandys, 15 December 1617. William Bradford, *Of Plymouth Plantation 1620-1647* (updated and edited by Samuel Eliot Morison; New York: Alfred Knopf, 1952, 2001), 33.

15. Spanish Queen Isabella, quoted in Federer, *America's God and Country*, 122.

Textbox Endnotes

Introduction

Page 5: Rush Limbaugh, commentary from TV program, 9 June 1994.

Page 6: Don Feder, *A Jewish Conservative Looks at Pagan America* (Lafayette, LA: Hungington House Publishers, 1993), 52.

Page 8: Nathan A. Forrester, quoted in the *Washington Times*, 24 December 1994.

Page 9: Pat Buchanan, "Hollywood's War on Christianity," *Washington Times*, 27 July 1988.

Page 10: Abraham Lincoln, quoted in Marion Mills Miller, ed., *Life and Works of Abraham Lincoln Centenary Edition.* (New York: The Current Literature Publishing Co., 1907), Vol. VI, 156.

Page 12: Andrew Jackson, quoted in William J. Federer, *America's God and Country: Encyclopedia of Quotations* (St. Louis, MO: Amerisearch, 1994 / 2000), 311.

Page 13: Daniel Webster, quoted in Verna Hall, ed., *The Christian History of the Constitution of the United States of America* (San Francisco: Foundation for American Christian Education, 1966 / 1993), 248.

Chapter 1

Page 17: Christopher Columbus, *Book of Prophecies*, quoted in Federer, *America's God and Country*, 131.

Page 18: Gary Wills, quoted in George Grant, *The Last Crusader: The Untold Story of Christopher Columbus* (Wheaton, IL: Crossway Books, 1992), 117.

Page 19: George W. Bush, quoted in "Lawmakers blast Pledge ruling," 27 June 2002, Posted: 1:11 PM EDT, <http://www.cnn.com / LAW CENTER>.

Page 20: Dennis Hastert, quoted in ibid.

Page 21: Kay Brigham, in Christopher Columbus, *Book of Prophecies* (trans. Kay Brigham; Ft. Lauderdale: TSELF, Inc., 1991), 23-24.

Page 22: Christopher Columbus, letter to Ferdinand and Isabella, quoted in Federer, *America's God and Country*, 121.

Page 23: Mark 16:15. *The Holy Bible*, King James Version.

Page 24: John Eidsmoe, *Columbus & Cortez: Conquerors for Christ* (Green Forest, AR: New Leaf Press, 1992), 48.

Page 25: August J. Kling, quoted in Robert Flood, *Men Who Shaped America* (Chicago: Moody Press, 1976), 13.

Page 26: Desmond Wilcox, *Ten Who Dared* (Boston: Little, Brown and Company, 1977), 13.

Chapter 2

Page 29: Leonard Bacon, quoted in Hall, ed., *The Christian History of the Constitution*. 23.

Page 30: Daniel Neal, quoted in ibid., 240A.

Page 31: Cotton Mather, *The Great Works of Christ in America: Magnalia Christi Americana* (Edinburgh: The Banner of Truth Trust, 1702 / 1853 / 1979), Vol. 1, 48.

Page 33: Paul Johnson, *A History of the American People* (New York: HarperCollins*Publishers*, 1997), 30.

Chapter 3

Page 37: John Palfrey, quoted in Hall, ed., *The Christian History of the Constitution*. 48.

Page 38: Cotton Mather, *The Great Works of Christ in America*, Vol. I, 79.

Page 39: Paul Johnson, *A History of the American People*, 40.

Page 40: Paul Johnson, ibid.

Page 41: From *The Holy Bible*, King James Version, e.g., Matthew 4:4, 7. Romans 3:10, 2 Corinthians 9:9, etc.

Page 42: "The American Church Manual," quoted in Mather, Vol. II, 199.

Page 43: Cotton Mather, ibid., 207.

Page 45: Cotton Mather, ibid., Vol. I, 80.

Chapter 4

Page 48: Paul Johnson, *A History of the American People*, 31, 46.

Page 49: Roger Williams, "A Plea for Religious Liberty," (1644), <http://www.constitution.org/bcp/religlib.htm> (31 January 2003).

Page 50: George Bancroft, *History of the United States of America, From the Discovery of the Continent* (New York: D. Appleton and Company, 1859 / 1890), Vol. I, 263.

Page 51: George Bancroft, ibid., 355.

Page 53: G. K. Chesterton, quoted in Os Guinness, *The Great Experiment* (Colorado Springs: NavPress, 2001), 70.

Page 54: One of William Penn's goals for Pennsylvania, quoted in Federer, *America's God and Country*, 502.

Page 55: William Penn letter, quoted in Catherine Millard, *The Rewriting of America's History* (Camp Hill, PA: Horizon House Publishers, 1991), 38.

Page 56: William Penn, quoted in Eleanor Doan, *Speakers Sourcebook II* (Grand Rapids, MI: Ministry Resources Library, Zondervan Publishing House, 1968 / 1989), 233.

Page 57: William Penn, quoted in Millard, *The Rewriting of America's History*, 38.

Page 61: Herbert Hoover, quoted in Federer, *America's God and Country*, 296.

Page 62: John Fiske, quoted in Loraine Boettner, *The Reformed Doctrine of Predestination* (Philadelphia: The Presbyterian and Reformed Publishing Company, 1975), 391.

Page 63: John Eidsmoe, *Christianity and the Constitution: The Faith of our Founding Fathers* (Grand Rapids, MI: Baker Book House, 1987), 203.

Chapter 5

Page 66: David Barton, *The New-England Primer* (Boston: Edward Draper's Printing-Office, 1690 / 1777. Reprinted by David Barton, Aledo, TX: Wallbuilders, 1991), 3.

Page 67: "The Old Deluder Act," *The Annals of America* (Chicago et al: Encyclopedia Britannica, 1976), Vol. 1, 184.

Page 68: Martin Luther, quoted in Robert Flood, *The Rebirth of America* (Philadelphia: Arthur S. DeMoss Foundation, 1986), 127.

Page 69: James Madison, Second Annual Message to Congress, Dec. 5, 1810, quoted in Caroline Thomas Harnsberger, ed., *Treasury of Presidential Quotations* (Chicago: Follett Publishing Company, 1964), 75.

Page 70: George Washington, "Farewell Address," *Compton's Encyclopedia* (Chicago et al: William Benton, Publisher, 1965), Vol. 15, 26.

Page 71: Cotton Mather, *The Great Works of Christ in America*, Vol. II, 9.

Page 72: Monsieur Guitton, quoted in ibid., 30.

Page 75: Timothy Dwight, quoted in Federer, *America's God and Country*, 222.

Page 76: Benjamin Rush, quoted in David Barton, *Original Intent* (Aledo, TX: WallBuilder Press, 1996), 153.

Page 77: Princeton motto, quoted in Federer, *America's God and Country*, 519.

Page 78: John Witherspoon, quoted in Hall, ed., *The Christian History of the Constitution*, 1B.

Page 79: George Washington to the Delaware Indian Chiefs, quoted in Barton, *Original Intent*, 85.

Chapter 6

Page 81: Samuel Davies, quoted in Guinness, *The Great Experiment*, 117.

Page 82: Paul Johnson, *A History of the American People*, 110.

Page 83: Jonathan Edwards, "Narrative of Surprising Conversions," quoted in Federer, *America's God and Country*, 224.

Page 87: George Whitefield, quoted in Peter Marshall and David Manuel, *The Light and the Glory* (Old Tappan, NJ: Fleming H. Revell Company, 1977), 244.

Page 88: John Wesley, "On the Death of the Rev. Mr. George Whitefield," Sermon 53 (text from the 1872 edition, 18 November 1770, Point #14).

Page 89: 300 Sermons by George Whitefield on John 3:3, found in <http://www.kprbc.org.sg/cw/CW_Nov12_2000.html> (21 February 2003).

Chapter 7

Page 95: Donald S. Lutz, *The Origins of American Constitutionalism* (Baton Rouge: Louisiana State University Press, 1988), 140.

Page 96: Charles Turner, quoted in Franklin P. Cole, *They Preached Liberty: An anthology of timely quotations from New England ministers of the American Revolution on the subject of Liberty: Its source, nature, obligations, types, and blessings* (Ft. Lauderdale: Coral Ridge Ministries, undated, c. 1985), 18.

Page 97: D. James Kennedy and Jerry Newcombe, *What If Jesus Had Never Been Born?*, (Nashville: Thomas-Nelson, 1994), 83.

Page 98: Franklin Cole, *They Preached Liberty*, 15.

Page 99: Franklin Cole, ibid., 42.

Page 100: Jonathan Mayhew, "A Discourse Concerning Unlimited Submission and Non-Resistance to the Higher Powers" <http://www.founding.com/library/lbody.cfm?id=230&parent=52> (21 February 2003).

Page 102: Jonathan Mayhew, ibid.

Page 103: Phillips Payson, Election Sermon, Boston, 1778 <http://www.lexrex.com/informed/otherdocuments/sermons/mass_sermon.htm> (21 February 2003).

Page 105: Minutemen Slogan, quoted in Federer, *America's God and Country*, 427.

Page 108: Jonas Clark, quoted in Cole, *They Preached Liberty*, 38.

Chapter 8

Page 111: George Washington, quoted in Barton, *Original Intent*, 156.

Page 112: *Compton's Encyclopedia*, Vol. 15, 29.

Page 113: George Bancroft, *History of the United States*, Vol. IV, 210.

Page 114: Engraving at the tomb of George Washington, cited in Federer, *America's God and Country*, 665.

Page 115: John Adams, quoted in Bancroft, *History of the United States*, Vol. IV, 212.

Page 116: George Washington, quoted in *Compton's Encyclopedia*, Vol. 15, 23.

Page 117: George Washington, quoted in Norman Cousins, ed., *In God We Trust: The Religious Beliefs and Ideas of the American Founding Fathers* (New York: Harper & Brothers, 1958), 55.

Page 119: *Encyclopedia Britannica*, quoted in Eidsmoe, *Christianity and the Constitution*, 247.

Page 120: Samuel Adams, quoted in Eidsmoe, *Christianity and the Constitution*, 255.

Page 121: Samuel Adams, "The Rights of Colonists as Subjects," 1772, in *The Annals of America*, Vol. 2, 219.

Page 123: Patrick Henry, quoted in Eidsmoe, *Christianity and the Constitution*, 307-308.

Page 124: Patrick Henry, quoted in Federer, "American Quotations."

Chapter 9

Page 127: Psalm 35 read in Congress, 7 September 1774, cited in Barton, *Original Intent*, 94.

Page 128: John Adams letter, quoted in Federer, *America's God and Country*, 7.

Page 129: Journals of Congress, quoted in Barton, *Original Intent*, 92.

Page 130: Massachusetts Provincial Congress, 1774, quoted in ibid., 427.

Page 133: Donald S. Lutz, *The Origins of American Constitutionalism*, 140.

Page 134: John Locke, quoted in Federer, *America's God and Country*, 398.

Page 135: John Locke, quoted in ibid.

Page 137: William Blackstone, quoted in ibid., 52.

Page 142: William Blackstone, quoted in Chief Justice Roy S. Moore, ed., *Our Legal Heritage* (Montgomery, AL: The Administrative Office of Courts, June 2001), 27.

Page 143: Calvin Coolidge, quoted in Harnsberger, ed., *Treasury of Presidential Quotations*, 20.

Chapter 10

Page 149: James Madison, quoted in M.E. Bradford, *A Worthy Company* (Marlborough, NH: Plymouth Rock Foundation, 1982), 147.

Page 150: Gouverneur Morris, quoted in Eidsmoe, *Christianity and the Constitution*, 188.

Page 151: Alexander Hamilton, quoted in Ibid., 428.

Page 152: James Madison, *Federalist #39*, Alexander Hamilton, James Madison, and John Jay, *The Federalist Papers*, with introduction by Clinton Rossiter (New York, et al.: A Mentor Book from New American Library, 1961), 240.

Page 153: James Madison, *Federalist #10*, ibid., 81.

Page 154: Alexander Hamilton, *Federalist #78*, ibid., 467.

Page 155: Donald Lutz, *The Origins of American Constitutionalism*, 85.

Page 156: Articles of Confederation, 1778, quoted in Bruce Frohnen, ed., *The American Republic: Primary Sources* (Indianapolis: Liberty Fund, 2002), 204.

Page 157: Catherine Drinker Bowen, *Miracle at Philadelphia: The Story of the Constitutional Convention May to September 1787* (Boston et al: An Atlantic Monthly Press Book, a division of Little, Brown and Company, 1966 / 1986), 89.

Page 158: Catherine Drinker Bowen, ibid., 140.

Page 159: Benjamin Hart, *Faith & Freedom: The Christian Roots of American Liberty* (San Bernardino, CA: Here's Life Publishers, 1988), 325.

Page 160: Traditional legislative prayers were approved by the United States Supreme Court in the case of Marsh v. Chambers, 463 U.S. 783 (1983).

Page 161: Bill by James Madison, cited in Hart, *Faith and Freedom*, 353.

Page 162: Nancy Gibbs, "Has the Separation of Church and State Gone Too Far?" *Time*, 9 December 1991, 62.

Chapter 11

Page 166: Romans 3:32. *The Holy Bible*, King James Version.

Page 167: George Washington, *The Daily Sacrifice*, quoted in Federer, *America's God and Country*, 657.

Page 168: Acts 16:31b. *The Holy Bible*, King James Version.

Page 169: Patrick Henry, quoted in Eidsmoe, *America's God and Country*, 314.

Index of Proper Names

Christian Law Association
PO Box 4010
Seminole, FL 33775-4010
www.christianlaw.org